REASON AND POLITICS

REASON
AND
POLITICS

The Nature of Political Phenomena

MARK BLITZ

University of Notre Dame Press
Notre Dame, Indiana

Library of Congress Control Number: 2020950365

ISBN: 978-0-268-10912-7 (Hardback)
ISBN: 978-0-268-10915-8 (WebPDF)
ISBN: 978-0-268-10914-1 (Epub)

To Ellen and to the memory of my parents.

CONTENTS

Introduction

This book's subject is the nature of basic political phenomena such as freedom, justice, and the common good. I wish to explore and clarify these phenomena but do not intend my effort to lead directly to practical results. I share the classical view that political phenomena are the heart of human affairs and central to understanding much that is not usually considered political. If we truly stand on the brink of transforming human nature it is especially important to illuminate what we seek to transform and what we may gain or lose in the effort. I intend my study to contribute to this clarification.[1]

To explore the nature of political phenomena is equivalent to exploring what is reasonable about them. "Nature" is the correlative of reason. It is what reason seeks to know about things, a view that begins with the classics and is still visible when we call the truths of physics and economics natural laws. I intend to examine the degree to which what we can uncover reasonably about political phenomena is not an adjunct to them but, rather, forms and directs them.

The "nature" of something is what in it we do not produce, what is common or pervasive in it, and what is essential to it. Our everyday use of the term attests to this. "Nature" is the environment and the species we do not make, and to be "natural" is to be spontaneous, not artificial and affected. Someone is said to have a calm or excitable nature, a characteristic that pervades his actions and is always present. The "nature" of something is its essence, what is always there that is important, not trivial, and that forms the thing's other characteristics.

Something's nature, therefore, also distinguishes it, as speech distinguishes us from cats.

This is not to say that the connection between what we make and do not make is transparent, that how characteristics can be common or pervasive is obvious, or that how essential characteristics function is clear.[2] It is to say that the natural as what is unmade, general, and essential is what reason qua reason seeks to know. Reason concerns primarily what we do not perceive physically, seeks what is general or universal, and separates and combines matters chiefly according to their central characteristics. As I said, reason is oriented to what is natural.

It may seem odd to seek what is naturally true about politics because politics is so conventional, structured by laws that we enact, dealing with passing circumstances, and variable in different places and times. Nonetheless, political life serves an understanding of what can be good, pursued by actions that are more or less just.[3] If what is good and just are natural and reason can know them, politics need not and, indeed, cannot be irredeemably conventional.

Politics involves what belongs to me and to us, as well as what is good or just simply. It involves what is particular and impure, however general. It involves freedom, passions, force, and prudence. The point, then, is to explore these matters in terms of how they are formed and directed by speech or reason, our unmade, pervasive, and essential characteristic. My goal is to bring out what is rational in what is contingent, or not simply rational, in us.[4]

The attempt to understand political life reasonably inevitably falls short. Matters are too complex to allow this attempt to succeed completely. One of my goals is to clarify the reasons for this complexity and for disputability in judgment and choice. We cannot measure all good things, including our own freedom, on a single scale. Nonetheless, we can judge matters reasonably, primarily in relation to the completeness of the use of our human powers.

Another goal I have is to consider rivals to my argument. One rival is the view that only what is mechanistic and mathematical about us is strictly speaking true. I will discuss this when I discuss freedom. The other is that reason itself is inherently contingent and particular. I will discuss this "historicist" view at various points in the book.

The Importance of Political Phenomena

Imagine that theoretical, philosophical, scientific, academic, and theological ways of understanding did not exist. How do they originate? In what phenomena are they rooted, and what calls for theoretical discussion? How do intellectual analyses still rely on and refer back to the phenomena from which they emerge?

We recognize, of course, that these ways to understand do exist now. Indeed, they often make it difficult to see clearly the basic phenomena from which they emerge.[5] We deal with terms such as "freedom," "property," "power," "justice," and "pleasure" as if they have always been matters of studied reflection. The variety in intellectual views, moreover, causes disputes that also block access to phenomena. Who today can look clearly at the relations between men and women, at whether human differences suggest basic inequalities, or at whether some activities are genuinely better than others? Who, taking such a look, feels free to say what he thinks? The twin results of our obfuscations—passive relativism and self-righteous self-interest—are visible, if themselves difficult to discuss honestly. These obfuscations also make it important to uncover basic phenomena clearly, including the possibilities of disagreement about them. Otherwise, they are lost to common understanding and to reflection.

We must also try to clarify the basic political phenomena because of the questions we face technologically: the growth of artificial intelligence and the effort to reduce everything human to the molecular and mathematical, perhaps, indeed, in order to make us over. Academics often discuss the distinctively human in terms of "consciousness" and relate these scientific elements to it. This points to the issue. But it also distorts it, for "consciousness" is already a remote way to approach what is human. It is a particular understanding that stems from a modern theoretical approach.[6] I will instead attempt to show that the original context of our activities is the political community, our involvement in common matters. Isolation of human characteristics, including who "I" am stems from this involvement. Exploring basic political phenomena is the first step in understanding human affairs.

The Political and the Cosmopolitan

Although the political contexts that form human phenomena are central to how we first see and deal with them, we must also account for what seems to be beyond political context, or cosmopolitan. A context's elements are suffused by the whole and are not merely detachable parts. Political actions and institutions in liberal democracies, for example, belong to the entire regime. One should not think of a country's institutions or laws as if they are simply separable from it and could be the same anywhere. Ignoring this often causes failed political reform. Nonetheless, a context's elements are not meaningful merely as its parts and nothing but its parts, with no possible independence. This is clear with physical and living objects such as trees and animals, which appear the same in democracies and oligarchies, in Athens and Berlin. Whatever the complexities involved here—stars that some view as gods, for example, species of trees that are unseen by most because they dwell on an aristocrat's estate, or animals unusable for unholy purposes—it is hard to deny that the tree noticed in one kingdom, its shape and natural reproduction, is largely the same as in others.[7]

Consider now courage and moderation. More clearly than with living and physical things, these differ with political context. Is it moderate to eschew the unholy allure of pleasure in order to stay on a righteous religious path? Or, rather, is it moderate to deal properly with pleasure considered as a good that inspires continued accumulation? Or is moderation, as proper enjoyment, noble in itself? These different views are connected to different political contexts and opinions about justice. They belong together with related views of piety, pride, freedom, and property. To what degree, however, can we nonetheless discover what is similar in these different instances of moderation? Is there not some comparability in pleasure as we seek, experience, and moderately control it, and in fear and courageously directing it, whether the control belongs to righteousness, bourgeois calculation, or classical nobility? To the degree this comparability exists we can consider each virtue on its own apart from its context and compare and perhaps even judge or rank its instances. In discussing basic phenomena I will explore the interplay between the dependence of phenomena on the whole or context to which they belong and the degree of independence that allows each to be addressed in its own terms. This interplay is the essence of human experience.[8]

My purpose is to clarify the nature of basic political phenomena. One problem arises immediately: how to begin? But is this problem not preceded by the question of why we should engage in the inquiry at all? A search for a missing suspect begins with clarity about who is missing and about why one seeks to find him, places to begin to look, and what counts as a successful result. If we do not know how to begin, perhaps our inquiry is unnecessary.

Presumably, we are unclear about basic political phenomena: the path to understanding and its beginning are connected to dispelling this initial unclarity. In what way are we unclear? For us today, unclarity on matters such as freedom and the common good is related to the complexity of our way of life, to our political partisanship, and to the variety of intellectual doctrines that we teach. What freedom is, is unclear because we dispute it politically and intellectually.

What, then, would end dispute or count as clarity? What would count as success? The questions of clarity and success, however, are themselves embedded in something still more original. For these questions are intelligible to us in some way. This original intelligibility is obvious when we look for a missing suspect (or a lost wallet) because there the intelligibility of losing, searching, and finding belongs to evident contexts of activity—to crime and punishment or to using everyday implements. The initial intelligibility within which unclarity about basic phenomena lies is the first clue to their meaning, because how we state and experience questions, unclarity, and the approach to dispelling them is embedded in this intelligibility.[9]

Perhaps, however, even "intelligibility" is disputed and unclear. Indeed it is, among philosophers. Martin Heidegger discusses ordinary intelligibility in terms of what allows us to understand how anything is at all. Plato connects our partially clear opinions to the true basis of intelligibility, his "ideas." Hegel displays the intelligibility of things through our step-by-step dialectical movement to what is completely and Absolutely so. Hobbes grounds facts on the experience of our senses, and on agreement about the names we use to designate things.[10]

The conflicting ways to ground intelligibility also indicate why a possibly indubitable or certain beginning may not be the correct starting point. For searching for and recognizing such a beginning also depends on a notion of intelligibility that we can challenge. And it is not evident that certainty is the appropriate goal for truly understanding the matters we are studying.

At some point what thinkers uncover must account for their own activities and discoveries. But when they begin they cannot start from their own completed views. Nor can they give evidence for their views or expect us to consider them true without confronting the ordinarily meaningful and intelligible. The most arcane physics indicates its truth about more than its own constructs by showing its useful or destructive effects in the ordinary world. My own inquiry concerns political phenomena, moreover, and these belong to everyday life.[11]

ORDINARY UNDERSTANDING AND POLITICAL CONCEPTS

For these reasons, I will begin from ordinary understanding and intelligibility. But which ordinary understanding? One characteristic of thought from Nietzsche forward is the attempt to root science, philosophy, art, and morality in a ground more basic than these activities themselves, yet not a physical-materialistic ground to which we can reduce everything. It is not mathematical physics alone that is fundamental but something equally or more central in which science itself is rooted.

This effort is behind the "life philosophy" and radical historicism that follow Nietzsche. It leads to Husserl's discussion of intentionality and the lifeworld, to discussions of the so-called natural world, standpoint, or horizon, and, especially, to Heidegger's analysis in *Being and Time* of human "being-in-the-world."[12] Although this effort culminates first in Heidegger's early analyses, it does not rest there. It continues next in Heidegger's further thought, and in that of his and Husserl's students, notably Leo Strauss and Jacob Klein. Problems such as the origin of philosophy, political philosophy, and modern mathematics are examined with Husserl's phenomenological standpoint and some of Heidegger's discoveries in mind.[13]

The result of these discussions is to recognize the importance or inevitability of beginning not from supposedly timeless yet in fact inherited concepts but, rather, from one's own immersion in one's own world.[14] Still, this beginning does not presume that thought must remain relative to one's time and place.

To begin from immersion in our own world is to begin from immersion in intelligible things and activities. This is less obvious than it seems. Some argue, instead, that we must begin from sense data, or material certainties.[15] This view is challenged powerfully by Heidegger, who argues, instead, that the things we uncover in significant worlds *are* as much as the material characteristics that seem to produce them. One of his best-known examples is our immersion in working with tools, such that each step is involved with the others and all are generally "ready to hand." Ready to hand entities are no less than the merely neutral ones we discover scientifically, from which they might seem to derive. A second example is his notion that a mood such as fear releases entities in their fearsomeness and that we cannot reduce their being as fearful to the merely chemical or physiological.[16] In Heidegger's view, our defining human characteristics are precisely those involved in our immersion in everyday worlds, and in the projection of possibilities that allow this.

Heidegger's understanding, however, is not the only attempt to begin from things as we deal with them. This beginning also characterizes Plato and Aristotle, something that Heidegger's standpoint and his approach to them help us to recognize.[17] I will attempt to develop our everyday beginning with attention to classical arguments in particular. I will orient my discussion to my theme: the substance of basic political phenomena.[18] But the need to begin from things as we deal with them, our reliance on ordinary practical intelligibility, shows the importance of grounding all our concepts in ordinary contexts and ultimately, I will argue, in political ways of life.

I will therefore start from our immersion in our own world and try to tease out from contemporary examples and directions the structural characteristics that comprise being immersed within an activity. My purpose is, first, to explore how human experience depends on context. It is, next, to show how particular activities and contexts belong to something common or whole that is characterized largely by the understanding of justice or righteousness that forms a way of life. Concretely, this means life within a political regime such as a liberal democracy or classical aristocracy or an orthodox religious way. Justice, moreover, embodies and serves an understanding of happiness, excellence, what is good, and what is appropriate. I will therefore explore how ways of life—political wholes—are constituted by how things first meaningfully approach us as choiceworthy, together with the justice that forms us. Each of our experiences comes to light within a meaningful activity; contexts that form meaningful action are linked by a political way of life; and the most significant political phenomena order, define, and are the central substance of this way of life and, consequently, these contexts.[19]

The coherence of contexts is not an intellectual superstructure we place over experience but is inherent in experience itself. Nonetheless, however close knit a way of life, it cannot encapsulate experience fully. As I suggested, we can observe moderation and courage somewhat apart from the orders within which we practice them. This separate view of the excellence of a regime's parts also allows us to question the justice and view of goodness that constitute it as a whole. This exploration, in turn, permits fuller understanding of the parts, the phenomena that belong to the regime.

This dialectic or spiral of the closedness of a way of life and openness to what is independent from it indicates the complexity of human experience, and the possibility of exploring matters theoretically.

Once explicit thought emerges we can see that basic political phenomena involve not only everyday intelligibility but also general and abstract matters. To comprehend practical affairs we must sometimes push forward to an understanding of ends, wholes, independence, movement, and other matters that we usually address philosophically. A community's parts, for example, can be common or separate in several forms: citizens can be identical, or they can vary by class. Good things can satisfy or complete in different ways. I mean to explore the place of several of these issues in understanding political phenomena. Much "abstract" understanding, in turn, generalizes from political opinion and experience. The place of theoretical issues is especially salient in liberal democracy, given our explicit basis in a notion of natural rights articulated by John Locke and other thinkers.[20]

I will concentrate on the meaning of practice, freedom, rights, power, property, virtue, goods, common goods, and justice. Because these phenomena are interlocking, I will discuss each in several places and not only in the chapter or section chiefly devoted to it. I will also address other topics that are salient to my arguments or appear to counter them. Among these are the natural basis of history, religion, and innovation; the relation between what is good and one's own; the possibility of ranking and comparing ways of life; and the place of reason in experiencing the passions.

Chapter One

The Nature of Practical Action

My first effort is to investigate practical activity and the place of context in understanding it. I wish to examine the power of the opinion that we live our lives primarily within what we take for granted and do not explore. This is the heart of views that understand us largely as creatures of history, identity, culture, and tradition—standpoints that can be intellectually serious and not merely assertions to gain political advantage. I intend to show the natural basis of such views while also addressing their limits by clarifying how we can recognize what is cosmopolitan from within particular ways of life.

Practical affairs are those in which we are engaged; that is, they are not affairs as we take distance from and observe them, except when observation belongs to the business itself. One way to understand the structure of practical engagement is to consider practical judgment. A related way is to consider common sense. Common sense involves being immersed in and making one's way around a context of implicit meaning and understanding, the preconceptual from which formal concepts are derived. It is what is missing in those who lack experience or judgment. It thus shows us what we take for granted implicitly as we conduct our affairs knowingly.

Knowing the context in which activities occur is crucial to judging and dealing with them.[1] What, then, is context, and how does one recognize it? What is the relation between context and practical action?

Practical activities involve action for reasons other than knowledge simply. Their goal is not knowledge for knowledge's sake. This is the obvious way they differ from theoretical inquiries. Most practical reasoning involves serving a purpose or meeting an end. A physician's knowledge means to restore or preserve health, or a shoemaker's to produce shoes. But reasons for action are not restricted to arts and production. They may also involve following a ritual or merely performing. One attends to the steps in order to do the dance, play the music, honor or respect the way of life. This attention can degenerate to mere ritualism or proceduralism, however, especially if it is detached from other goals such as pleasure or beauty.

Practical activities also involve knowledge or recognition that is embedded in the activity itself. This is one reason experience often matters practically. This embeddedness is especially evident in situations whose outcomes are not guaranteed. If one is negotiating, for example, one is persuading and cajoling, not merely observing, and it is useful to be able to recognize the effect of moods and other changing factors on the negotiation's status. These factors include reactions to the situation as one is shaping it. A policeman needs to be able to gauge the likelihood that actions or situations might be criminal or whether threatening or dangerous behavior will actually explode. He needs to see how much his own actions and inactions might bring about the result he wants. A physician needs to be able to recognize what symptoms mean, that is, what they tell us about health and disease, and she adjusts her judgment as she learns more.

MEANINGFUL THINGS

What is involved in such practical recognition? The central point is that we are seeing meaningful things. One counter-notion, as I said, is that we first see and deal with the least complex, simplest, and most universally present impressions and then work our way up from them. Is it true, however, that we first see neutral or detached colors, quantities, and shapes that we then compose into things? Rather, in practical activities we usually first see things such as guns or wallets; the times when we see or hear mere detached impressions are unusual.

It is also the case, however, that we sometimes do not see things such as guns or wallets but, rather, mere bulges in someone's pocket— not impressions to be sure but, nonetheless, objects with minimal qualities. The next counter-notion to my claim would be that we usually see these, that they are basic and that we build up from them. Yet objects such as bulges that may look identical when detached from their surroundings for academic inspection usually call forth a variety of reactions within their surroundings, even seen as mere bulges. In a dangerous situation the bulge in the pocket might be a gun. What we deal with or react to practically is the gun's presence or absence; if we see the bulge we may worry or wonder what it means. The bulge is, practically or actively, a potential gun. In other situations we may simply not focus on it: it has no importance. The "mere" bulge is in fact noticed in particular situations, each of which when we attend to it would show the bulge to be something specific and not a mere bulge. A cough may sometimes be just a cough, but in other situations we worry about what kind of cough it is. Is it a fearful, guilty, or disease-ridden cough? The notion that the neutral quality is what is always there first is in fact often untrue: it is either an abstraction from what is more meaningful or something present only in particular circumstances. We can arrive at the neutrally measured dimensions after the fact or notice them at particular times. But it is not such neutral dimensions or impressions that we normally first deal with and notice. We could never build up from such "data" to fuller phenomena or devise a rule to do so unless we recognized the fuller cases on their own (as other than the data) in advance.

It seems, then, that it is more reasonable to work down from the full things that we notice in ordinary contexts to the less complex rather than try to build up to them. Yet it is also clear, as I said, that the neutral bulge has some degree of its own meaning. This seems even more obvious with a cough, where explanations of its origin may appear to be separate from the thing itself.[2] Moreover, one could often show that the things we usually deal with and see, guns and wallets, say, are themselves reductions, connected, for example, to proper use, ownership, and production or to appropriate defense or destruction.[3] The issue, then, is both to understand how ordinary practical experience works at the level of meaningful things and to see where these things and this working can be meaningfully expanded or reduced.

The Contextual

What more can we say about what we recognize and deal with practically? To discuss this I will further examine contexts and the contextual. For what differentiates one bulge, cough, or hesitant action from another is an activity's context.

The context answers the question, what are they doing, or what is happening? It involves the interrelations of the activities to which one is attending or in which one is involved. This involvement or attention demarcates a context practically from its surroundings. Crucial in practical recognition, as I said, is the reason for the activity. The interrelations among the things to which one is attending, which are largely ordered in terms of their purpose, are what constitutes the context. The "sense" (or common sense), that is, the total practical sight that one has of this combination of the purpose and the matters linked or interrelated with it, enables one to see what is relevant or important among specific actions. What one names or calls things brings out this relevance and fixes it.[4] In this sense, we can notice the context through any of its elements. A context is primarily the nexus of purpose and activity, with the substance of context being the order of activities, their when and where. Not understanding what is happening means that one notices some or even all of the elements without their "why"—their purpose and connections—being clear or notices that some familiar steps are out of order but not the reason for this. So, for example, what is happening in a store or laboratory is opaque if one has never been in one before, and even an expert can be confused when hearing a misplayed musical piece. Is it poorly played, jokingly played, or intentionally disruptive?

Let us further consider not understanding. What does the bulge in the pocket mean? Within a context it is mysterious in a relevant manner. It might even illuminate the context or show that one did not grasp it fully. Things that appear to have no meaning in fact often are occluded in specific ways: one does not know for what the tool is being used, why the odd clothes are being worn, or why something is being said. That is, they are partially familiar, largely because of related contexts. This also suggests that some things (and not merely stripped down characteristics such as mere bulges and coughing sounds) have an average (and not merely stripped down) generality that one notices across contexts — plants, animals, human beings, and so on. But such generally present things enjoy much of whatever rich meaning they have from the contexts of practical action to which they belong and what we remember about them from our increasing understanding of them.[5]

IDENTIFYING CONTEXTS

How do we identify the contexts in which we are immersed, in which we act, or on which we concentrate? Consider the following example. A policeman is asked to identify suspicious activity in order to prevent a crime this activity might be indicating or to arrest the perpetrator. How does he know which activities are suspicious? He sees odd behavior in a blue car: it is parked on a street corner for a long time, different people are coming and going from it, the driver and passenger never walk far from it. Is this behavior suspicious enough to be worth investigating? Should the driver and the passenger be frisked to see if they have weapons? Will the police officers be reprimanded if they uncover no direct evidence of crime?

The first issue here is the unclarity of what counts as suspicious activity. One cannot be certain of this: truth about much in practical affairs is not "certainty" in the Cartesian, mathematical, or scientific sense. Often, it is not certainty even to the everyday practical degree that one knows, say, that the door to a house is now closed. Other clues tell us still more about context. Has there been drug activity recently in the neighborhood? Is the car the kind that dealers favor? Has one received advance warning of criminal activity? Do the people who approach the car approach furtively? The context of the activity is important in judging what the discrete elements of behavior (which we could interpret in various ways) mean in this case.[6]

If one suspects that the activity involves buying and selling drugs, because of warnings, telltale actions, or one's experience, then all the activities fit together and make sense. Taken separately they could mean many different things. Even several of them taken together could mean different things: furtive discussions about planning a crime could instead be about challenging a union head, breaking away to start a new company, political action, or even planning a celebration. These goals, however, are less likely than drug sales to explain all the actions (and prior warnings) or be indicated by them.

Some things in a context are clear: in my example, a blue car is standing at the corner. Often what is obvious makes the context evident to anyone who is otherwise prepared to understand it: they are using this ball so they must be playing football. Rows and rows of blue cars are standing here so I must be in a factory or on a dealer's lot. (If one is not otherwise prepared, however, these clues do not help.) But often what is unclear and needs interpreting within a context is the key to understanding it. I see shifty behavior: what is motivating it, and why, at the same time, is the car standing so long on the corner? The largely neutral events—the car is blue and is standing still—do not tell us enough. What is missing in my understanding is recognizing in advance the meaningful order in which both the usual and the unusual stand.

CONTEXTS AND MEANINGFUL ORDER

What is "meaning"? Meaning's two fundamental elements are intelligibility and guidance. We might ask, what does "radio," "justice," or "snowstorm" mean? To give a meaning here is to make the term intelligible by pointing out what it describes. Or we might ask, why is he doing that—kicking the ball—and what does it mean? Why is he making that move? In this case, the meaning of something is also its intelligibility: the meaning of the action is the rational fit that allows it to be intelligible. A meaning is an explicable or rational fit for something or some activity: he is making that move because. . . To give or to know a meaning is to orient or direct, as one might say of signs or surroundings that they mean nothing, that is, that they fail to orient: they are unintelligible as not orienting. So the meaning of something is what is intelligible about it, largely as orienting or directing, or showing something's place or relevance in an activity.

We see a second element of meaning in the following examples. This antique means a lot to me, is dear to me, is connected to me, and it brings back memories. Something's meaning here tells us what is important about it. Or we can say that this thing or action is meaningless, petty, trivial, unimportant. A meaningful relationship is one that is compelling, engaging. Something's meaning, here, is how it affects one, how it compels or engages. We also speak of man's search for meaning, or say that having a child gave her life meaning or direction and makes her other actions meaningful. Meaning here is purpose and direction. Meaning also involves what one holds on to or devotes oneself to: it's all meaningless, empty, we might say. What is meaningful is also what matters or counts: it shouldn't mean anything, one might say, it shouldn't matter, but it does. So, taken together, meaning, here, is what affects, draws in, compels, engages, connects, or guides (as a purpose does.) And this guiding purpose then or concurrently puts things in order, allows them to be explained or described, fits them together, directs or orients them, points them out so that they stand out. (What is the point, i.e., the meaning, of this activity?, one might ask.) By directing, orienting, and guiding, meaning allows matters to be divided and combined: a meaning is intelligible and allows further intelligibility. So, taken as a whole, meaning is guiding, orienting, intelligibility—hence its connection to justice and goodness.[7]

Practical judgment and common sense involve understanding meaningful things. But, above all, they involve understanding not only things, but the actual order, connections, and true purpose that are implicit in ordinary tasks, and recognizing this order prior to or concurrently with noticing the things with which one deals. Common sense means knowing what comes next and what likely came earlier, when and where an activity ends and how it likely began.[8] It involves seeing, noticing, or intuiting here and now the order in which things happen, the likelihood of their happening, and which actions matter.[9] Intuition, or "having a feel for things," is not only of separate things, but of situations. Common sense means knowing what ambiguous actions, statements, and emotions likely mean, what their correct place or fit is in an activity, how much weight to give to certain steps or actions, and why they may indicate that "something else" in addition to what seems visible is happening. It also usually involves a general understanding of motives, capacities, and likelihoods that is broader than the current situation, at least within the overall range of typical activities.[10]

Context and Politics

This points to the next feature of contexts and practical judgment, namely, our normal expectations about others' usual behavior. The substance of these expectations varies, but recognizing some kind of reliable behavior that people follow or ignore is significant in recognizing and acting within a context. Here I have in mind the general sense one has of others' trustworthiness and reliability, the character and ordinary practices one implicitly expects and on which one depends in business, politics, and elsewhere.[11] (I do not mean simply abstract motives and behavior.) These general characteristics are constituted by "our" habits, virtues, character, and practices, the approaches and dispositions on which we rely (and, therefore, about which we can be disappointed), the actions that we expect to take place, and the areas where we expect only limited compliance. These characteristics constitute the expectations we have of others and the general and specific reputations on which we rely and in which we trust. They are related to practical opinions about proper behavior and to the reigning public opinion.[12]

Understanding the place of expectation is the first step in showing how any context relies on something still broader. Reliability, reputation, and character both set and emerge from expectations about proper behavior. Consider, for example, an ordinary context of buying and selling, or hiring someone to work at one's home. One has implicit expectations about responsible behavior—honesty, doing the work on time, helpfulness, and so on. In buying and selling, these expectations help set the boundaries of action. With major transactions we use explicit contracts but do not need them when we purchase items in a supermarket. We permit half-truths from automobile dealers and in antique stores but not in pharmaceutical sales. These expectations also set the boundaries for observing or noticing contexts— what we consider ordinary behavior and where we need special wariness because we see something out of the ordinary. "Out of the ordinary" means other than, or a break in, the usual path of activities.

Although I mentioned responsibility, which is a liberal virtue, reliability and reputation are not limited to modern communities, to an explicit understanding of character, or to law that commands or restricts behavior. Our own way is our usual first example, however, and even broad terms such as reliability, expectation, reputation, and trust may seem limited to it. Nonetheless, others' reliable actions within one's way of life, one's trust (or lack) in them, are a necessary part of any social, political, or religious order.[13]

Let me consider further our contemporary case. Business, medicine, entertainment, and teaching work within a setting broader than their own limited activity. Common sense and practical reason within these activities are connected to and trade on our general expectations, trust, and reliability. These expectations are sometimes codified in law and sometimes not, but they are always present. Beyond but connected to virtue and character, moreover, is our view of equal liberty, equal opportunity, and equal access. This view affects how we first see others and our understanding of who can produce or obtain what. The reputation, trust, and character on which we rely are appropriate to this view of equality and fit or fail to fit it in specific ways. Similarly, there is an implicit sense of purpose and good that is appropriate to our activities.

The understanding of equality and liberty changes to a degree. As I will argue, this is the heart of change in our "culture." Still, such change occurs within our overall liberal view of what is good—of goodness—as what satisfies desires and can be pursued equally in an economic market.[14] Class distinctions grounded in law are inappropriate. In general, and without ignoring the fact that class or regional differences occur in fact, a wide practical horizon of liberal democracy is implicit, reflected, and largely embedded in specific practices and contexts. The usual practical whole or order within which specific contexts reside is the political regime—in our case liberal democracy and the expectations and character connected to equal rights and opportunities—or the religious and traditional ways (the righteous ways) that precede civic regimes.

The basic dimensions of the other phenomena that I will be discussing are connected to and framed by context: our experience of them and their intelligibility emerge within contexts of common sense and practical judgment that rest within the political order, the way of life.[15] We cannot separate explicit theoretical concepts from their origin in such orders and experiences, structured and organized as I have sketched them.

I have said that the way of life, the regime, which is the broadest practical context of implicit understanding or meaning, is composed from a sense of goodness and justice. The implicit understanding of what allows matters to be good, to be choiceworthy, their goodness, directs how ends and means, purposes and actions, first and primarily present themselves as acceptable. There are several possibilities of such "goodness." Goods can present themselves as relieving unease, which, as I have said, is the heart of liberal democratic or bourgeois life; as available for virtuous or noble choice or as present for specific pleasures and satisfactions, which is the heart of classical aristocracy and democracy; and as allowing continued proceeding along a righteous or pious path.[16]

The implicit understanding that constitutes the meaning of ways of life involves more than a view of what can be good. It is also linked to an implicit sense of justice, of who is permitted to perform which actions and enjoy and produce which goods, following which procedures. Justice concerns an understanding of distribution and of the interrelation of actions, individuals, and institutions that allows them to fit while retaining some independence. The justice of possibly just acts and laws is how they present themselves as fitting within a whole.

Broadly, they are modes of equal to equals and unequal to unequals, combined with a view of the degree to which citizens and activities can be independent.[17]

The justice and goodness of a way of life involve an implicit and sometimes explicit understanding of similarity and dissimilarity, of holding, seeking, and possessing, of what counts as common, complete, and separate, and of movement and direction toward sufficiency. These "ontological" matters may not exist intelligibly apart from things and actions, but we cannot reduce them to things and actions. They provide a basis for comparison of ways of life and of their elements—that is, for what is cosmopolitan about them. Our movement is always both temporal and elevated and is oriented to being complete.

CONTEXT AND CULTURE

A further way to consider context and the priority of political regimes is to examine the phenomenon of "culture." For we often call our ordinary expectations matters of culture. Rapidly changing expectations—about careers and family life, say—cause much of the uncertainty and discombobulation that occur in everyday life. Culture, however, also involves art, music, and thought, either serious or popular. It concerns intellectual matters as well as habits and mores.

We also see this duality when we consider the connection between culture and education. "Culture" is related to growth—agriculture, horticulture—and human growth, the soul's growth, is both moral and intellectual. The difficulty this dual use hides is that a good moral education may differ from a good intellectual one. The areas of similarity (the need for "discipline" in both, for example) should not disguise the areas of difference—the need in one but not the other, say, to be unconventional and, even, irreverent.

Moral Culture

We sometimes talk about corporate culture, gang culture, and the culture of poverty. "Corporate culture" refers to whether a business is hierarchical or freewheeling, centralized or decentralized, or has a daily atmosphere that is relaxed or strict. It concerns how we develop attachment to the firm—through "love" and paternalism, through fear, or hardly at all. "Gang culture" refers to much of the same: us versus them; who leads and who follows; proving loyalty; camaraderie and care. The "culture of poverty" involves how we form expectations about what is right and wrong, proper occupations, and our own capabilities.

If we distill these meanings, we see that culture indicates matters of rule, loyalty, hierarchy, and independence, largely in private life. It also refers to expectations about how to live and what goods to choose: what kind of person am I, and what is good for people such as I? So much that we call phenomena of culture are actually phenomena of justice, or of justice and love: who should do what, for and with whom? This is one reason the issue of culture is so much the issue of family.

In all these areas, "culture" refers less to general understanding and more to the embedded expectations that we usually take for granted. It is precisely these embedded and meaningful expectations that constitute contexts and that link them in a way of life. Culture in the moral sense refers to how embedded expectations about a regime are expressed here and now in our particular affairs.[18] Indeed, this immediacy is one reason culture often seems to involve historical variety. (The other chief reason is variance among artistic and philosophical works in different places and times.)

As we use it, then, culture in the (expanded) "moral" sense refers to the current intersection of one's character and opportunities with the reigning public understanding of proper rule and the proper distribution of goods. "Culture" points to goods and opportunities insofar as an embedded understanding of justice and choiceworthiness allows, disallows, and ranks them, especially privately. The ground of our culture is the reigning notion of who deserves equal amounts of what, the expectations we have of others' character connected to this, and the dominant notion of what goods and good lives we can and should choose.

Culture and Opinion

One reason equality and liberty are so important in American culture is that opinions about them govern what we can say respectably. Serious intellect must attend rhetorically to the publicly respectable; for the less serious, it is what we cannot see beyond. Our movement in the United States has been toward converting equal natural rights to equal civic rights and then toward equal or identical treatment of others privately as well as publicly. "Liberty" becomes simple self-assertion, with a diminishing grasp of its original limits, conditions, and justification—its connection to pride of ownership and economic growth (rather than to oligarchic accumulation), to industriousness, responsibility, and toleration (rather than approval), to earnest faith, genuine art, serious thought, and science, and to political deliberation. Public discussion is increasingly governed by a presumption in favor of the identical respectability and availability of all modes of living that do not question this equal propriety. Such notions make proper distinctions difficult to state and defend publicly: distinctions are seen only as assertions of power.

This difficulty with making reasonable distinctions also means that a vacuum occurs into which assertions of special status thrust themselves, publicly by various groups or more quietly by those who seek to maintain oligarchic privilege. The result is our peculiar current American combination of growing egalitarianism, the rise of assertively intolerant groups, and the attempt by some to freeze in place their unequal status and wealth.

This growing current view of what freedom and equality mean is based on but distorts or revises our original opinion and helps set the immediate horizon within which character and expectations develop.

Intellectual Culture

On its own, the question about today's intellectual culture is whether serious nonscientific thought and the status of quality in the arts have largely declined. Taken politically, the question is how this decline, if it is present, affects the country's political and moral health.

It seems evident that there is indeed a decline in intellectual and academic rigor, which results both from our weak understanding of virtue and from developments internal to the arts and thought. It is difficult to discuss excellence, and, thus, to recognize it, and, thus, to muster the integrity to seek to emulate it. This fog then leads to art and teaching that exacerbate the problem morally and politically.

The moral and political context, however, does not simply control arts and thought. Arts and thought partially transcend any political order because they stem ultimately from a love for truth, beauty, justice, and what is good that no political context or community can capture fully. We tend now, however, to believe that thought and arts are cultural "products" and that all artistic cultures are equally arbitrary. The grounds of this view are intellectual and rest largely on Nietzsche's thought. Everything is said to stem from historically variable structures of domination—inescapable assertions of willful overcoming.[19] Indeed, our assertive moral egalitarianism is extended by academic acquaintance with such Nietzschean arguments. In this sense, the moral and the intellectual in our culture largely reinforce each other's difficulties—rather than limiting and controlling them.[20]

The heart of moral culture is the way of life, largely organized politically, that forms the expectations that define more specific contexts. "Culture" names the current implicit and sometimes explicit interpretation of a regime's original sense of goodness and justice, and of what from within the choosable it is "today" considered best for me to choose. The everyday expectations in our American way of life, for example, change largely because of the actual spread and effect of free self-direction—say, to former slaves, new immigrant groups, and women. This change is properly inherent in the meaning of liberty. But cultural change is also shaped by the growth in education and law of misunderstandings of liberty and excellence: we increasingly confuse equal rights with equality in all things, and come to believe that we can overcome technologically everything that limits enjoyment.

Our culture is thus a defining element in our particularity but neither as ineluctable history nor as mere material for our liberal democratic form. Rather, it is how we today understand liberty, equality, responsibility (and other virtues), and what is good—what these are, who enjoys them, what (and how stable) our expectations are, and what I should now choose, given this. The original liberal view of justice and what is good remains central in our regime; changes within this view are the heart of changes in our culture.[21]

The Nature of Political Openness

I turn now to several phenomena that indicate the possibility of opening to what is beyond one's way of life, that is, to what is cosmopolitan, while still being embedded in the basic context one implicitly takes for granted.[22]

As I am arguing, it is too restrictive to understand being immersed in a context only as absorption in narrow tasks. Rather, immersion exists within a political horizon of reliability and trust. This unity partially helps us to account for the remarkable fact of our quick shift in attention within activities and to different types of activities. Rather than believe that each new activity comes from nowhere, as it were, it is more likely that each is first available and meaningful in the whole to which it belongs.

Moreover, some possibilities appear to be natural, or cosmopolitan. So, for example, we are observing children playing at the table at one moment and paying half or full attention to a Beethoven concerto the next—or concurrently. Indeed, even what might be forbidden or "unthinkable" within one's way of life must nevertheless enter understanding to be forbidden in the first place. Awesome fear or power may limit the effect of deviance from the norm, but it cannot expunge all its attraction: to educate is to see something of the range of what one tries to control.[23] A common intelligibility exists that grounds many of our rapid shifts in attention.

We may also explore in these terms the role of explicit knowledge and skill in practical activities. Much that we do is implicit. But some things can be taught, shown, discussed, and described. The classic examples are arts such as shoemaking, piloting, and medicine. Such knowledge compounds experience and technique. Where others are at sea one, instead, has a clear sense of what steps will bring about a useful result and how to manipulate material and situations to achieve this. We may think of an art as systematic or methodical common sense. Its methodical elements enable it to be effective beyond particular ways of life.

The place of reason and discussion is still greater when we choose an activity's time and place, or whether to perform it at all. Many actions, say, military ones, require prior deliberation and explicit judgment. This discussion—the statesmanship that guides military affairs—cannot help but consider what is best for one's way of life. It must therefore gaze beyond it while remaining within it.[24]

The most significant ordinary political experience that opens beyond one's own regime is political founding, or making constitutions.[25] Here, the activity's very meaning involves an openness to justice or the right way and its links to what is good generally. One goes beyond what one takes for granted and must consider broader evidence. Founding institutes a form and an end that derive from what is general, even if not simply understood. In classical political regimes the presence within any one regime of the kind of partisanship that Aristotle discusses—the split between rich and poor, above all—keeps this basic awareness active.

INNOVATION

For most activities, one prospers by taking one's political horizon for granted and acting narrowly within it. Nonetheless, innovation occurs. Discussing this will help us to see further how communities are open to natural justice and excellence, a narrow opinion about or version of which they usually assume.

One way innovation becomes possible even in the most traditional communities involves the necessities of defense in war where the goal, victory, may override traditional limits and activities.[26] A second involves the press of desire, however controlled, when it comes upon the foreign and attractive. Novel particular pleasures as well as pleasure generally may announce themselves as possibly choice-worthy. In both cases, innovation means separating the good—for example, the good result—from the just or the traditional way. In some cases it also involves beginning to separate one's self, one's own, from our way. This beginning may not be developed, say, in a pious community where the tie between one's self, our own, what is righteous, and what is good is so close that the separation required for judgment hardly exists. But the lure of pleasure and the danger of war mean that the possibility of exploration is possible nonetheless.[27]

A third natural start to innovation involves having a deeper or more general sense of the activity in which one is involved while still taking for granted its worth and propriety: putting a subject on wider grounds allows one to uncover new elements in it. Plato's *Statesman* discusses modes of repelling and compounding that let us see new uses for old materials, and Plato likens statesmanship to weaving, medicine, gymnastic training, piloting, architecture, and other arts, thereby clarifying the range of its powers. Innovation rooted in such generic understanding and likening separates matters from their immediate context and materials and illuminates new goals and actions. The statesman not only restores the body politic's health; he strengthens it. He not only guides the ship of state; he commands his helpers. He not only employs one art; he weaves the virtues of several. He not only weaves citizens' skills; he binds them to common laws and opinions. He not only protects by covering and warding off; he defends actively.

These kinds of generalizing and likening are one way that concepts, as explicit foci of understanding, arise and vary. A second way is through exploring, comparing, or defending the opinions and practices that help to constitute the justice and goodness of a way of life—as a founder or statesman might. A third is to look back at political regimes in terms of ends, wholes, separateness, commonality, and the like, that is, to look back from the ontology they implicitly project. Changed practice based on such thought is broadly intellectual, but it need not all be explicitly theoretical.

HISTORICISM

To see that the central political concepts emerge from phenomena that are embedded in ordinary practice does not demand a classical standpoint. On the contrary, such embeddedness might suggest the importance of traditions and history, as I indicated in my discussion of culture. Indeed, one might claim that we are tied ineluctably to our present situation until what is new somehow emerges. Our current way of life and anything significant that might change in it are not, in this view, natural possibilities but temporal and particular ones.[28]

One argument supporting this view is the claim that we sometimes find or produce possibilities so novel that we could not have seen them earlier. What we newly discover, moreover, brings previously unimaginable results. Modern science is an example. A second major instance is said to be Christianity and what it reveals about human beings—the phenomena of guilt, sin, and love, for example.[29] More broadly, some claim that fundamentally new drives and passions emerge, and with them new views of the just, good, and true.[30]

These new possibilities occur randomly in some views and in other views are ordered.[31] The new may reveal itself fully from the start or, rather, require further enactment to be present and grasped. So, as Hegel argues, there is a substantive order in history, but we see only a partial version of things until we reach history's end. Indeed, one might even claim that what is new is fated to emerge "now." A historical view may also hold, moreover, that from now on there will be nothing truly new, as Hegel apparently believes, or that there can be significant new discoveries, as Heidegger thinks, but that the truly obscure and important matter (for Heidegger, being) has finally begun to be understood.[32]

The substance of what historicists claim to be newly discovered areas seems largely to involve religious views of monotheism and its human effects; different and novel philosophical understandings; natural science and its mathematical basis; "history" itself; new directions in art; and, perhaps, the individualism of natural rights and self-consciousness. The serious question, then, is how much here is

new and how much develops what is visible earlier, although unde-
veloped. From the ancient standpoint, the issue is whether we can
grasp in classical terms what "history" seems to uncover. Perhaps we
can explain the source of religion sufficiently naturally.[33] It is especially modern mathematics and the natural science based on it that
seem new. Yet are they simply novel as human possibilities? And are
not their concrete results what distinguishes science from mere games
and formalism? Would science be important if it did not affect health,
transportation, and communication as we see them with our own
eyes—that is, as we can comprehend them prior to modern science's
actions? On the other hand, do not the modern philosophical enterprises fail to grasp as well as the classics what the classics uncover
ethically and politically, what they see in terms of the soul, and how
they understand the origin of philosophy?[34] The natural explanation
of embeddedness, novelty, and openness, some of whose elements I
have indicated, is the heart of a confrontation with historicism: it is
not evident that we need to account for what seems to be new in historicist terms.

HEIDEGGER'S "HISTORICISM"

An alternative "historicist" way to consider our immersion in contexts of activity is Martin Heidegger's discussion of "factic" life, his
description of immersed particular existence. From it he develops his
radical understanding of human being. Our central characteristic, he
claims, is how our own being is an issue for us, not intellectually, but
as we proceed in the most ordinary ways day by day. The fact that
how I am to be is always an issue for me is unavoidable. Heidegger
then develops his understanding by stretching out to the experience
of the elements and horizon that make such factic life possible.

It is not the abstract generality of these elements that is central,
however. What is central is that we always already exist in a world of
meaningful things; "worlds" are Heidegger's version of what formally
or more narrowly I described as contexts. Our activities, he argues,
are grounded in the possibilities that we are for the sake of. These

possibilities are given us by the people and generation in which we reside and are ordinarily given to me as one among others, as a "they-self." I can, however, transform myself into what is truly my own. I can be authentic, once moods such as anxiety show me my irreducible responsibility for meaning, once I anticipate the possible end of my possibilities in dying and thus see how possibilities are unavoidably mine, and once conscience and guilt show me the possible nullification of any possibility. I can then be resolute within the current situation: this resolve also illuminates public possibilities, so that the public becomes an authentic people.

Questioning Heidegger

Heidegger believes that my possibilities are always transmitted in a historically limited fashion and are presented to me in terms of what "they" say, do, and choose. But is not what I or we should choose, what is good for us, open beyond what has been brought forward to my here and now? One cannot intelligibly state what human openness and immersion mean (which Heidegger intends to describe) without discussing the direction or happiness for which we are open. What attracts me, my pride, and the attempt to use my powers fully do often belong to my immediate realm of choice. But they also carry their grounds beyond me in a manner that detaches me from here and now (myself and us) at the same time that I am immersed in them.

Some sense of what is guiding is indeed projected in advance of choice. But the substance and approach of what is good are not merely a heritage in Heidegger's historical sense. Rather, we also inherit an understanding of goodness and satisfactions that seeks to account for all that can be choiceworthy. Our movement is not only horizontal or historical but vertical, too, and always incomplete because I and we are oriented to the cosmopolitan. What is good is substantive, attractive, compelling, and guiding beyond finite heritage, and this cosmopolitanism belongs to its "inherited" meaning. So my and our enclosure in meaning and context is not absolute. Any country or culture is a regime, an example of a just order, as well as being or belonging to a particular people. Every regime limits certain possibilities. But it cannot do this simply: what may be good or just more generally announces itself.

Heidegger attempts to see us as the very ones that we are now, the one who I am during this time as opposed to being an instance of a scientific or theoretical generality, the one within this occasion, the one now thinking or teaching. He tries to lay out the characteristics of this one, who is not a bare subject or consciousness with attached predicates or qualities. He then develops our authentic individual openness in terms of guilt, anticipation, and possibilities' historical transmission through the public or people. But one could also treat my possibilities and choices as deflections of a more general goodness, justice, and self. I experience my pride and virtue not only within this here and now, but as more generally and intrinsically choosable. That possibilities first approach as temporal does not mean that they approach only in a manner encapsulated within my people and myself. They approach also as more fully or completely realizable in ways that guide me beyond and, perhaps, against the current order.

This generality is also true communally, that is, also true for political choice. We are "up" as well as out in our possibilities: we attempt to consider possibilities as separate from our culture, and attempt to consider our regime's justice in relation to other regimes. We are never only just the ones we are here and now, and our movement shows this. Heidegger's connecting all our possibilities to a particular people rather than also to what is more cosmopolitan than (and may conflict with) my people is an important intellectual ground of his support for the Nazis. In contrast to Heidegger's view, the "temporal" properly includes the aspiration to perfection and completeness; it includes what I will examine in what follows as the erotic as well as the spirited.[35]

CONCLUSION

Four major points emerge from my discussion of the nature of practical activity. First, it occurs within a context, and contexts largely exist as the purposes and orders that form and direct what we expect. Second, contexts and expectations are implicitly extended to the regime or way of life in which we live—for us, liberal democracy—and the character, virtues, or pious ways it promotes. Third, the way of life is formed by the approach of what allows things to be good—their goodness—and the justice that seeks to achieve goods. This similarity of ways of life in terms of their being formed by meaning allows us to compare and, ultimately, rank them. This comparability is one ground of conceptual understanding. We can also explore how modes of movement, completeness, separateness, and commonality are implicated in this justice and goodness. Fourth, however unified a regime is, so that freedom, virtue, enjoyment, and other elements are connected in it, it nonetheless cannot be strictly rigid. We can attempt to examine its elements and activities on their own. This is another ground of conceptual understanding. These points will be a basis for my further discussions of political phenomena.

Chapter Two

The Nature of
Freedom and Rights

I turn now to freedom. As with other phenomena, the issue is how we experience it, how we understand it, and the link between experience and understanding. As I have argued, it is best to begin with our own situation. So let us consider typical contemporary uses. I am free to see you now. I am not free to talk at the moment. I have some free time. This seat is free. This upgrade is free. Free love. He is free to speak his mind. Feel free to give as much as you'd like. He is free to sign with any team he wants. He is a free agent. He is free to do what he wishes. Free verse. Free throw. I am free of that responsibility. He has been freed from prison. Free at last.

The general meaning of these uses of freedom is to be unencumbered, unburdened, unoccupied, unchained, unbound, unhindered, unimpeded, unrestricted, undetermined, uncommitted, not obliged, let loose, released. This is one basic experience of freedom: to be unburdened, unrestricted, undirected, at ease, open. This experience can become one of being lost, at sea, or at loose ends—discombobulated rather than poised for action or choice. This is freedom experienced as a burden rather than freedom as being alleviated, expansive, and unburdened, let alone experienced as good.

What we experience as freedom, however, is not only to be un-hindered or unencumbered. Consider being forced to act, made to do something, compelled by a greater power or authority: I acted under duress; I had to practice; I wasn't free to ignore his pleasure, her concerns, her needs; I felt I had no choice; the devil made me do it. Here the experience and understanding of freedom is not to be unblocked and unhindered but, rather, not to be compelled: we experience and understand freedom here as not being forced, or as acting spontaneously. To be free is to be self-directed, self-motivated, self-activated, even if one obeys others willingly. To be free is to choose, consent, or elect, on one's own. Together, then, we understand and, especially, experience freedom as being unhindered and uncontrolled or, to put this "positively," to be open, at ease, expansive and, also, to be poised, in control, ready, self-directed, or self-activated. Freedom is openness for and together with self-direction and self-binding.

Freedom's openness and self-direction occur in relation to activity and thought and the intelligibility that makes these possible. If freedom is openness for taking action, one can understand it only together with actions that have a certain scope and length of time. Self-direction, thus, is not merely not to be directed by others. It is also not to move arbitrarily or randomly, or not to be battered from side to side. Freedom involves a length, steadiness, or degree of self-direction and unhinderedness. This is why discussions of free will can be too narrow to comprehend freedom, because one also must uncover what self-determination and nonhindrance are poised/open/unburdened in terms of or for, over time. Freedom involves self-direction but, also, staying on and following a path—for example, of thinking. That is, it involves self-binding. Otherwise, it is mere arbitrariness, even if it seems to be one's own arbitrariness. But one must also be able to leave the path.[1]

Another central experience of freedom is its necessity. It is unavoidable for humans even if one seeks to avoid it. To be free is a necessary or essential component of what we are. This apparent paradox is vital in experiencing and understanding freedom and connected to its occasionally seeming to be burdensome.

NEGATIVE AND POSITIVE FREEDOM

The two major elements of freedom are similar but not identical to negative and positive freedom or freedom from and freedom to, common ways to understand it.[2] To be unhindered or unencumbered is similar to negative freedom. But to be unencumbered is not merely to be released. Rather, it is also a positive state of openness connected to a positive state of readiness. "Negative" freedom, moreover, does not clearly enough distinguish between being unhindered and undirected and being flighty or unsteady. We can fully clarify hindrance and self-direction only by also bringing to light the actions and goods toward which we are directed or in relation to which we are hindered. This is evident in the examples of freedom one implicitly has in mind while analyzing it. Furthermore, analyses of "positive" freedom usually mention particular types of action that alone are considered free. Typical examples are determining oneself to follow Kant's moral law or Rousseau's general will. Yet self-direction or motivation does not as such mean determining or binding oneself in one of these ways. So discussions of positive and negative freedom and of freedom to and from are incomplete.

FREEDOM AND MASTERY

Let me develop my formal discussion. Does every hindrance or limit to immediate self-direction restrict freedom? Is all "independence" actually free? Or might it sometimes hide a subtle hindrance or lack of self-direction. Most of us, on reflection, would say that not all hindrance to immediate self-direction restricts freedom: one restrains children or holds people back from crossing streets when they do not see oncoming cars. But why does this not restrict freedom, given that one's self-direction is being immediately limited and one's action is being immediately restrained?

Every training or educating restrains. It restrains so that one learns to improve or master. What one now masters increases freedom because one can do or enjoy more, well, and because one's range of action is less hindered—more open. Still, when one is being trained one is being hindered at the time. Who, then, is being restrained and whose mastery and open possibilities are being increased? Oneself and one's powers. Yet not all training is equally important because not all powers are equally worth developing or all goods equally worth enjoying. We must ultimately understand compulsion and restraint to operate for the full or whole soul or self in relation to goods and fields of action properly understood. This includes the time and breadth required to enjoy the goods and pursue the actions for which we are free. Liberal education liberates from domination by others and by error and opens or loosens the often unrecognized restraints to one's thought and choice. Liberalism does this generally by loosening the restraints of poverty and class. While one is being liberally educated, however, one may believe oneself to be restrained.

The degree of self-mastery is linked not only to the powers of the soul, as we are suggesting, but also to the breadth, depth, and extent of the goods or activities that are the object of enjoyment. The goods one feels, experiences, and enjoys are linked to the soul that masters them.[3]

FREEDOM AND LIBERAL DEMOCRACY

In thinking about or experiencing freedom, as I have said, one implicitly has in mind a particular good, or group of goods.[4] Experience is never simply "an" experience isolated from context. The experience of freedom is similarly connected. When my implicit example of being free is to think a thought, satisfy a hunger, or act justly the free action involves an implicit movement, permission, and satisfaction, a whereto and completeness.

To further clarify freedom we must therefore consider goods and the common good more fully in order to grasp toward what the soul's full movement, its direction, unencumbered readiness, and attentive binding are oriented. The primary point is that freedom is related to things' meaning and availability—their goodness and justice—and, then, to their concrete accessibility.

Activities in which we might engage or things we might choose approach us meaningfully. They first guide and are intelligible in a certain way. Freedom is our movement and direction toward and un-hindered immersion in accessible things, together with our movement toward and unhindered immersion in their initial and continuing intelligibility and guidance, that is, their meaning. The approach and the movement are correlated. An end or goal is not isolated but appears in a general presence or attraction, and we understand ourselves in a manner correlated to this. For us in liberal democracies, for example, things approach as possibly equal goods to choose or enjoy, and they approach equally for all.[5] Any "satisfaction" is temporary and partial, so choice and desire move restlessly among their objects, which satisfy desire (where desire is seen as unease), relieving unease and gathering strength or power in that relief. The breadth of our possibilities in liberal democracies may disguise this initial narrow universality, this initial meaning of our liberal goods. And immersion in a particular activity may hide this first movement and approach. Nonetheless, the flat possible equality of satisfaction is the first approach of "good" things, and restless, calculating, unease is what first gathers itself for self-direction. The theoretical background of liberal democracy makes this clear as does our economic market, in which in principle and to a large degree in fact things are ignored in their other qualities in order to be equal matters of buying and selling.[6]

From this point of view, free political institutions are those that serve the free and equal self-directed attempt to satisfy desire. They do so by securing the conditions for this satisfaction, by limiting government to this goal, by employing and enhancing the character I need to execute and secure my freedom, and by advancing self-government. The notions of goodness and of the soul that experiences goods in liberal democracy explain the importance of these concrete institutions in liberal freedom generally. Indeed, this liberal sense of freedom also forms our freedom of religion and worship and of speech. As with freedom generally, freedom of speech means both not to be restricted in one's speech—not to be hindered—and to direct or control one's speech. Ultimately, however, the worth and true freedom of speech is connected to the excellence of speech or reason and is not limited to liberal political freedom. Rather, it points to liberal education.

FREEDOM AND INTELLIGIBILITY

If we consider the initial meaning of goods in a context or way of life, the initial way they are intelligible and guiding before any particular choice, we see that we must locate freedom in its coordination with this meaning. The gatheredness for and openness to meaning—to what is intelligible to us and can guide us—is freedom: poisedness or readiness for self-direction and moving (including thinking) unhinderedly in this meaning. The unavoidability of some openness and immersion is the necessity in being free. Freedom in this broad sense is the experience of gatheredness for . . . , openness to. This is the heart of, or necessarily co-present with, self-determination and being unhindered in relation to particular goods and actions, whose intelligibility and choiceworthiness would otherwise be opaque.

My mention of powers of soul and unhindrance in satisfying desires suggests the standpoints of classical and of modern liberal thought. But to understand freedom does not depend on these standpoints. For freedom concerns not only the classic soul or the one who holds rights but also the transcendental will in Kant, Hegel, and Nietzsche, and Heidegger's *Dasein*. The elements of "soul" in these accounts are not classical powers, and their objects are not classical goods. For the classics, unlike the thinkers oriented to the will, the abilities of soul have full or proper natural uses and objects. Those of the transcendental self, however, are linked to what they productively shape or to that in which they are freely immersed as material to shape. Full freedom is tied to openness to and directedness within the realm of what is most pervasive for the will: the self-effected moral ought or Idea for Kant, what we can re-create and overcome for Nietzsche, or always fated being for Heidegger. Still, freedom in each case is poised self-directed and self-moving immersion in what is (for these thinkers) most open or available.

My account might also suggest that we cannot compare forms of goods, and their initial intelligibility—that they are sealed contexts. As I have said, however, grounds of comparison exist. The meaningful context and way of life is the first basis for how the things with which we deal address us, but we can to a degree treat them independently and not merely as parts of a whole. So, for example, we experience pleasure in liberal democracies primarily as the satisfaction of desire seen as relief from unease. This understanding is connected to liberal democracy's other elements. Liberal democracy as a whole can be questioned, however, and we may also uncover pleasure in many of its other qualities when we try to examine it alone or seek to restrict it. To then emphasize these other qualities is implicitly to see pleasure's meaning and effect in different, nonliberal, ways of life.

To be free means not to be blocked, hindered, or interfered with and to be self-directed, to stand in openness or availability, gathered or poised to direct oneself or directing oneself to the degree needed to deal with the activities at hand.[7] We first stand and move within a meaning, a "goodness" of possible goods as they approach us, and a context of justice, of distribution, trust, and expectation that allows them to be produced and enjoyed. We normally take this context and meaning for granted. We usually do what we do immediately and directly; we do not explicitly consider the intelligibility and mode of guidance of the good things with which we deal, which we assume in moving toward or being satisfied with them, or even consider explicitly the fact of our freedom in relation to them. The private and public spheres of free action in liberal democracies, for example, are usually just there, just present. Nonetheless, we sometimes do bring freedom more directly to our attention—when something for which we wish is unavailable, when we are interfered with, when ordinary expectations about actions and who performs them change (i.e., when culture changes) and we can no longer easily direct ourselves, or when we explicitly consider the institutions that support free action.

Is Freedom Possible?

To fully understand freedom I will need to explore more fully both the motions of the soul and what is good. First, however, I will develop our understanding by turning to other issues.

If freedom means self-direction, not being hindered, being open and unburdened, one must ask whether it can exist if humans are determined by that over which we have no control. We often raise this question as the impossibility of free "will" if material "nature" determines us. A powerful statement of this difficulty comes from the claim that the material cause of things operates with necessity. And because we belong to the material world and cannot be apart from it, everything we do is completely subject to material determinism and predictability. As our material understanding of human action becomes more concrete, this argument becomes more powerful. The issue is an especially acute version of how to grasp properly the connection of "consciousness" and other human characteristics to their material (or as is now often said, "physical") conditions, because material causality seems to make free will a nonbeing—not even an "emergent property," as is sometimes claimed, but an illusion.[8]

I do not mean to engage the large literature on this subject or the nuances of determinism, predictability, and causality.[9] Rather, I intend to use this question to clarify further what freedom is.

It is useful to remember that many claims of determinism do not depend on material determinism. They also arise when one believes that everything is historically, divinely, psychologically, sociobiologically, or economically predestined. We should also see that the issue does not exist only for the will, because, as I indicated, the "will" in the modern sense is not the only possible ground of freedom. It is also useful to remember that the usual, direct, practical question at issue involves criminal blame.

We begin with that point. Criminal blame occurs in a context of everyday responsibility for action, and we should first discuss the possible illusion of freedom at that level. This is why claims about poor upbringing, poverty, and need make sense: they make it more difficult to obey the law. Difficult enough to excuse the criminal's action? This depends on a variety of factors: the urgency of the action, the difficulty of obedience, the degree of criminality, the needs of society, and so on. If someone completely lacks the possibility of accountability, moreover, this may not excuse action but, rather, require confinement.

One might then suggest that factors of upbringing and situation apply in some measure to everyone. More directly, if our actions are materially determined this determinism applies to everyone. Everyone's action would then be excused, and none would deserve praise: the whole notion of blame, credit, punishment, and excuse would be senseless. But if this is true, to whom is one addressing this point, with what expectations? If we all must do what we must do, then I must punish, blame, excuse, or praise as and whenever I do. This makes the notion that there is an action that I "should" take because I am convinced that a criminal's behavior is inevitable and therefore excusable because of material causality odd or contradictory. If, however, material causality still allows me to be persuaded and to choose, why not others, too? One might then say that material determinism applies more to some than others, but this is merely a claim until justified, and it allows free will or free action in any event. So it is more reasonable, if one wishes to differentiate among those who are justly and unjustly blamed, to point to the factors mentioned above whose influence may indeed be variable and which to some degree would excuse crime by, say, making judgment about proper action very difficult—because one does not grasp the just alternatives, is unable to take them seriously, reasonably judges criminal action to be better in the situation, or is simply overwhelmed by pleasure or pain. But this differs from the universal excuse that material causality would offer.

A second beginning point is to consider arguments about historical, religious, or economic determinism. If one knows or believes that God has determined the world's course and one's place in it, or that one's class, race, or gender determines one's actions, or that one's stage in historical development causes or limits action, then how can one act freely? Why should one bother to choose? One conclusion from such thinking is passivity: one will necessarily wind up this way or that, whatever one does. But why should passivity be the result? Why not activity or even excess, if that is how one is disposed? Indeed, although the outcome might be determined, one might not know what this outcome is and, therefore, would still need to choose one's actions. But what if one does know the outcome? Then perhaps one does not know one's own place in the path required to secure the result and, thus, would need to choose one's way. But what if one does know one's place? Then one may see that it is precisely one's own efforts that are required, and these may be or seem to be efforts of thought, judgment, and action that present themselves as choices or options. Unless one knows in advance the path and outcome, one's place in bringing it about, and each step-by-step element of one's effort, then one's own actions still present themselves as needing to be chosen. Central to the fated outcome would still be one's own knowledge and effort. This freedom is not an illusion because in the reality of one's actions choice is still salient. In general, moreover, one cannot fully know a path or outcome in advance if one's knowing affects this.

Let me now develop the argument from another direction. Sociological, economic, or psychological causes such as emotional states appear to exist at a level of meaningful complexity similar to our choices of ends, goals, and activities. But when we have in mind predictable and inevitable physical actions we are at a different level of inevitability, and it is difficult to make the notion of determinism at some molecular or particle level square with being determined at the full or human level.[10] The grounds of intelligibility are too different. One cannot (or cannot yet) even fully describe what happens in thought, virtuous action, or complex emotion at the molecular level, let alone show how it determines the other. Indeed, we hardly have an adequate account of human thought and action themselves such that we could say what conditions or "determines" them. Moreover, one might ask how the truth of a true statement could be determined chemically or how what is good could be determined when one engages in complex judgments about the common good. Making the statement and expressing the judgment might conceivably be determined but not their meaning or intelligibility as true, good, beautiful, ethical, and so on. Actions whose virtue, goodness, or truth is what motivates, activates, or provides the reasons for them, and which are therefore good, virtuous, or truth-seeking actions, cannot as such be caused materially, although they may not exist without the material. The issue is not or not only "consciousness" as one way to understand "I," "my" experiences, and judging objects in relation to this, but any intelligibility or experience of the soul, subject, transcendental I, self, or *Dasein* and what it stands in and opens toward.

I can make this same point even more directly. Physical or physiological facts cause other such facts, but in what way can they cause what is grounded, motivated, approached, and understood in a different manner? The virtuous act qua virtuous act has meaning apart from and no meaning strictly in terms of the material, which is at best a condition of but not equivalent to the motive or ground of what we must describe and approach in another way. For the virtuous choice to be, say, chemically determined, the determining elements would themselves need to be the choice—courage, friendship, or magnificence molecules, as it were.[11] Even the chemistry that seems most associated with, say, conditions of attachment or aversion is involved with but cannot as such define virtuous and vicious friendships, or courageous or cowardly flight.

HEIDEGGER'S ARGUMENTS

Arguments to this effect are made with special force by Heidegger, who discusses freedom often. Ultimately, his analysis rests on his understanding of the connection between man (*Dasein*) and being. We can understand our characteristics in terms of our openness to being, not in a narrower sense. This openness, in turn, belongs to our temporality or finitude, the fact that we are not eternal or outside of time but always project a future, bring forward a past in doing so, and are immersed in a related present. Resoluteness in a moment that projects the possible nullity or ending of our possibilities in dying reveals through guilt the limits into which we have been thrown and, in anxiety, strips the immediate meaning from activities in which we are engaged—all these together can reveal our authentic being to us. Our freedom is ultimately to decide to stand in the openness in which beings present themselves and to be responsible for revealing entities in their meaning and truth.

We can also grasp Heidegger's understanding of freedom through the issues and distinctions I am discussing. Freedom means not being bound and self-direction. It also means binding ourselves to a direction under which we have placed ourselves. This is what I have called the steadiness of self-direction: nonarbitrariness. Such freedom does not center on episodic freedom of the will in the usual sense, although will properly understood must belong to freedom. Freedom is also not mere indifference, because self-direction always already posits in advance the possibilities toward which it is inclined. Moreover, it is not merely the faculty by which we choose what is good but that by which we choose good or evil, that is, choose in advance that which binds them together as possibilities.

Heidegger develops these views of freedom through analyses of Kant and Schelling. Ultimately he means to show that freedom from, freedom for, self-determination, self-legislation, and standing within and freely choosing good and evil are grounded in the free openness to being as he understands it. We are not able to escape from our freedom and ourselves.

Heidegger and Mechanical Causality

As I am arguing, the question of freedom also involves the issue of our apparently being caused mechanically and, therefore, seemingly being unfree. The experience (or feeling) of freedom cannot, in Heidegger's view, be reduced to mechanical causality any more than we can so reduce our other human characteristics. Our characteristics are meaningful as articulated and connected through language, as allowing us to understand the nonperceptible, and as they distinguish us from animals. Ultimately, indeed, causality belongs to freedom rather than freedom being merely an illusory version of causality. Heidegger writes, "Determinism denies freedom, and yet by denying it, it already must presuppose a certain idea of freedom . . . as noncausal, as an a-causal occurrence. Therefore determinism . . . remains outside of freedom from the start. [That is, it still sees it in terms of causality.] Freedom has nothing to do with causality. Freedom is to be free and open for being claimed by something. This claim is then the ground of action, the motive. It has nothing whatsoever to do with causal chains. What claims . . . is the motive for human response. Being open for a claim lies outside the dimension of causality." Determinism, or knowing the causes "cannot say anything about free-dom at all."[12]

To say this in related terms: "Motive calls forth free will. It does not restrict it." "Motive is the ground for acting this way or that, for moving oneself for this or for that. Ground does not mean an efficient cause here, but it means a 'for what,' 'the reason for.'"[13] Heidegger's view of the difference between physical cause, which is an ontological determination of nature narrowly understood, and the ground of the human (which is not restricted only to his view of motive) is also clear here: "If electrical impulses were really able to cause moods, then a machine alone and by itself should be able to produce moods. It can only be said that when electrical impulses are present this or that mood appears. However, this is far from saying that an electrical im-pulse can produce a mood. Mood can only be triggered. . . . A certain brain state is correlated with a particular mood. Nevertheless the brain process is never sufficient for understanding a mood; it is not sufficient even in the most literal sense because it can never reach in the mood itself."[14]

In general, we must recognize that "in this domain one cannot *prove* anything. One must abandon the belief that only what can be proved is true. There are matters, like presence or freedom refusing any claim of measurability here. We are . . . dealing . . . with insight into what we ourselves always already are."[15]

WHAT FREEDOM PERMITS

One corollary of this discussion is that although we discover many physical facts that predate man, these facts are not all that is domi-nant. As I have said, they do not cause virtuous choice or other free human actions. Indeed, that things, including scientific discoveries, have meaning as earlier and later is also inseparable from human beings or our rational discovery. The full power and meaning of the earlier and in this sense the causal is not separable from man, from what is later. Human conceptual understanding, our seeing and de-veloping matters, is necessary to bring out the full powers even of what precedes us. This is obvious with what we produce, but it is also clear with what we do not produce yet reveal in its fullness, or develop in novel situations.[16] Resources such as oil are not "resources" until we develop them as such.

One result of these points is that, because of the irrelevance for choice of believing all outcomes to be determined, current and future arguments about determinism should not affect one's practices. Actions performed as free should continue apace. Another point is to see that recognizing and understanding what freedom and determinism mean is itself a meaningful action that does not occur mechanically but, rather, at the level of organized and free complexity. We must first allow things to appear to us in natural scientific or technological terms, we must first project them this way, we must first uncover them in these possibilities, if we are to understand and develop what is true about them in these terms. This suggests that the full presence of scientific truths and of what they can bring about occurs only together with free human understanding, however conditioned.

THE LIMITS OF FATE

Still another element of the question of determinism concerns the limits to what mechanism (or fate) can bring about, looking backward from meaningful action or presence. If certain complex meaningful matters are truly necessary or impossible, nothing physical could determine them to be otherwise. Consider mathematics and geometry. What is true in them might rest on assumptions more variable than once thought, and we may put old truths in larger contexts, but we cannot make them false when true. Is this because their material basis limits and determines all outcomes or, rather, because one cannot materially cause what is not possible? That this is truly virtue, say, or that beauty directs or restricts the beautiful things that we can produce limits our actions, no matter how powerful our mechanisms.

Perhaps, however, such substantive limits are only in the mind, are only how we must see or organize things, and this is materially caused? This, however, is a merely speculative view. When justice means equal to equals and unequal to unequals, certain distributions are just and others not. It is hard to see how the meaning and fact of this just distribution are caused by the power of what the material can effect or condition rather than limiting and in that sense directing the material. This suggests the incomplete reduction of the meaningful to the material and the independence of the meaningful.

Let me consider still another related issue here, namely, openness and possibility. Essential freedom of choice is coterminous with recognition of possibility. Meaningful recognition and choice are not only of this or that thing or class of things but of things in their possibility of being chosen and of our directing ourselves toward them. (These are elements of their meaning, of their intelligibility and how they are involved in guiding us.) This openness and possibility mean that one is always seeing or experiencing more, and farther out, than one is experiencing immediately. Even if one claims that a choice or action is conditioned or somehow determined, difficult as it is to say just how the material becomes the meaningful, it is hard to see how what is there but not there—particular possibilities not yet imagined or seized to which we are open as possibilities—can be determined now.

We can also notice the link between this point and my discussion of context and ways of life because contexts are central to recognizing things as meaningful, formed, as they are, by an intelligible order and expectations and by goods or goals seen in their goodness. Contexts of activity and their opening to ways of life always contain "more" than is available at any time.[17]

FULL FREEDOM

The fullest experience of freedom would involve recognition of and unhindered immersion, explicit directedness, and lingering movement within the fullest context, the fullest ends and intelligibility.[18] This criterion is also coherent with the fullness of the "I" that is free as open, light, unburdened, ready, and self-directed. The full unity of the elements of freedom is the philosophical life and its openness to the whole of things, or, to a lesser degree, the experience of political greatness of soul or of the full responsibility of the liberal statesman, with their immersion in and directing of complex political orders. Freedom of thought is the distinctive self-direction and unhinderedness of our distinctive capacity. Freedom of speech is a vital condition of thought because our self and self-direction require options beyond what we are likely to discover merely by ourselves. Liberal education is at its best the coherent presentation of discussions that allow thought to place itself within its proper field.

FREEDOM, MOTION, AND THE SOUL

I turn now to a brief discussion of the movement or motion inherent in the experiences of the "I," the self, the soul and its powers. If freedom involves not being hindered and directing oneself, it is connected to types of movement. The movements I have in mind are human or meaningful movements, not those that we can measure neutrally apart from their meaning and context.

Modes of movement and related modes of fitting, separating, combining, and opening are central to freedom, rights, and other phenomena. They are ways to characterize the elements of the "soul" in its various forms: the classical soul; the Cartesian or Lockean "I"; the Kantian, Hegelian, or Nietzschean will; the unique authentic self; and Heidegger's *Dasein*. Variations in these modes of soul and what satisfies them are central to understanding different ways of life and political-philosophical views. In discussing movement we implicitly have in mind certain goods to and from which we are moving.

To experience self-direction is to experience (and implicitly understand) movements (pushing, pulling, following, restraining) and satisfactions (ends as stopping, resting, burgeoning, completing, organizing.) It is also to experience the related openness, expansiveness, readiness, closedness, and resistance. Not only do we first see and experience things (rather than sense data), but we also experience these elements of human movement, in ways connected to different contexts. The concepts of understanding formalize the intelligibility implicit in such experiences. They are not inventions we impose on static material or things.

Kinds of motion have always been fundamental in understanding. Grasping motion explicitly is basic in Aristotle and Newton's physics. But matters are less clear political-philosophically. Still, references to the importance of falling, directionality, immersion, and projecting (reaching out and extending) in Heidegger, to restlessness, disquietude, or incompletion in Tocqueville and Hegel, to unease in Locke, and, especially, to eros and *thumos* (spiritedness) in Plato show the importance of motion or human motion generally.[19] Examining satisfactory, noncontradictory, completed, and authentic (or resolute) motion is a way to capture the different philosophical experiences of the soul.

It is not difficult to list modes of movement. This is useful in understanding activity generally. Let me consider first several everyday varieties. We rise up and sit down. We push, reach, pour, extend, pull, and gather in. We run toward and away, go forward, around, back and forth. We move along or stand still. We shake, tremble, stabilize, and stiffen. Each instance of a type of movement, moreover, does not differ from others only by degree. We rise up restlessly, calmly, energetically, lethargically, quickly, and slowly, for example. These adverbs may indicate a common measure, so that the quality differs by amount, but they may not. Whether we move too calmly or energetically, or too quickly or slowly, for example, varies with activities and circumstances.[20]

As I am suggesting, our movements do not merely concern physical matters. They also, or primarily, involve matters of politics, soul, and thought and do so not (merely) metaphorically. We long for someone or something, a parent, child, lover, home, work of art, or understanding; that is, we wish to move toward or embrace it. We show forward movement in our sales and marketing—we show progress. We belong to, oppose, or are indifferent to the women's movement or the communist movement, that is, to a political cause: the cause impels movement or attracts it; the movement may march forward or may shake things up, to change or destroy them. Someone moves up or down in his work or moves on or out. Others are movers and shakers. Someone moves restlessly back and forth waiting for something to happen or for news about what is happening. We say that a symphonic movement is finished, completed, ended, over, that a performance, event, or piece is moving. We claim that a speech moves or does not move us. "I'm unmoved by his plea." We bristle or stiffen when our pride is attacked, thrust things away, shatter, overcome, incorporate, or possess them. Our actions begin with or are characterized by our "motives."

These uses suggest that human movement is meaningful. This is true even when we change our place: I move my residence or march forward. And forward movement can also involve activities that are even less physical than this—sales, as I said, or work on a project or piece of art. We cannot successfully measure such movement neutrally, as is clear when we consider forward movement to be "progress," which it may not be. This is even more visible with other movements. Consider being moved by a symphony—say, by the first movement of one of Mozart's later symphonies. We experience an out and back and fast and slow but also a being suffused, an embracing, a gathering: we speak of our "emotions." Or when one understands something (quickly or slowly) one moves and continues to move forward and around and see how to combine things or separate them.[21] Freedom as self-direction can involve each of these movements of the soul, and its objects. Central are the emotions that suffuse and can (along with reason) "motivate" forward and back, separating and combining things as one journeys toward a completion or satisfaction.[22]

The free movement of the soul is oriented to things in their meaning—what is good about them (their goodness) and our expectations about their availability, that is, how one can move or proceed toward them, how they can be distributed, and their possible independence.

LOVE AND SPIRITEDNESS

The first basic movements of soul that are significant for freedom and action are eros, or love, and thumos, or spiritedness. Because the soul exists as a unity immersed in activities, however, to separate its different elements in order to examine them inevitably distorts them. We must keep this in mind as I develop the discussion.

Eros and thumos are central in the first philosophical discussion of the soul, in Plato.[23] Eros is love. Love is needy: it reaches out and puts together, or combines. We think of attraction, sex, the couple in love, two parts of a compound, a whole. This reasonable way to understand love, however, forgets something equally evident. For if we consider being attracted to the one with whom we are in love, it is as if they are perfect, untouchable, put on a pedestal, a goddess as some say. Eros is needing or desiring, but it is also observing the beautiful, the perfect, the wonderful. Here eros wishes to be together with the one loved, not to incorporate, use, or join with it as if it has no independence but, rather, to be together with it as the very thing it is. In fact, self-admiration also exists: when this admiration is not illusory it is a ground for seeking to improve oneself and properly employ one's skills; it may even involve trying to live up to the perfection or excellence another sees in you.

I bring up this phenomenon because our reasonable attention to the couple, coupling and what is common in love, can overlook how love loves the independent or exquisite, that is, not a part simply to be joined in the couple, the whole. Love is a movement, a reaching out, that needs what is missing and joins in a whole, but it is also an admiring, a living up to the perfection one admires and wishes to be with. Eros transports or uplifts and does not merely combine.

In combining, love also places apart or differentiates: a lover distinguishes the one loved from all others, then the lovers distinguish themselves, the couple, from (or even against) the others, the world. In love one becomes oriented to or absorbed in the combination, the couple, the common, us, we two. Nonetheless, love cannot be completely self-forgetting: proper eros seeks to join with things while allowing them and oneself still to be what they are. Indeed, love can produce something new, ours but also independent, a child, and can continue to combine. The more love combines elements, joins them in a new common or whole while still allowing differences—while still allowing the precious and exquisite and elevating oneself to this—the more love fully displays its power and excellence.[24] Love's orientation to perfection as well as to combination, to the beautiful as well as to the needful (and, therefore, ultimately to all things brought together in their perfection, if possible), means that it can move from something that seems complete to what is more complete, from us to family and to community, and from what is to its still better or more beautiful instances. So, for example, love of someone beautiful displays love's elevating and combining power less completely than love of noble action for one's community or love of the beautiful simply.[25] Understanding is aided by love's combining: it follows the path of something's (say, beauty's) increasingly complete appearances as it shows its power in wider, higher, or more pure spheres and, therefore, shows itself more completely.[26] Indeed, love is oriented to likeness and likening, similarity, perfecting, but also to the wholeness of what it brings together and joins and, therefore, to the different, the complexity in the whole and within the parts, the exquisite and unique in what love combines and has combined. So eros tends to join each beautiful thing with beauty simply while also dwelling on each instance as itself "perfect," and to combine something beautiful and beauty itself with other things into a family, city, or cosmos, and to see or elevate oneself in relation to these. Thus the first evident object of love is the one loved and then this couple and our child.

Spiritedness is also a movement, a movement of separating, identifying, protecting, and, even, withdrawing. It is the movement we associate with anger, pride, and self-defense (and hence with rights, as we will see, for rights are grounded in reverence for what is inviolable in oneself). Its proper political outcome is to defend courageously what it separates, if it is just and good. Spirited courage in battle to protect a just community, moreover, is a fuller courage than is courage in business, let alone in shadow boxing. As separating me or us, it can also then incorporate others, say, after victory in war, unifying or absorbing them into one rather than combining them into a common (a whole), with separable, potentially whole, parts.

Spiritedness's characteristic vices are improper separation — excessive fear and the loss of one's own independence, or excessive anger and the destruction or agglomeration of the hitherto independent. Its excessive or vicious political outcome is conquest and tyranny. Ultimately, spiritedness may wish the dominance of oneself alone, one's name, what one does not share. Others are merely competitors to be overcome, incorporated, or destroyed, not perfected: they are identical as "other."

When eros supports understanding it tends to see things in their wholeness: to differentiate wholes and elements in wholes as complete, as perfect, but also to see how they combine and might further be combined—how they are alike. Spiritedness, when it supports understanding, tends to see things as recalcitrant, unyielding, perplexing single units and necessities. But it may then overcome this closedness to understand how to absorb or agglomerate them into a more expansive unit or one. For each is identical as other. (Intellectual examples of this agglomeration are mathematics, the modern conquest of nature, and manipulating things through methodologies alien to their own ways.)[27] In eros's progress in understanding, it accompanies the attempt to see an idea such as beauty at work with the matter and in the field of its fullest combination and combining power. In spiritedness's progress in understanding, it tends to see things in the area of their fullest availability for agglomerating and manipulability, overcoming or conquering their closed independence. When the dialectic of the movement of eros and spiritedness accompanies thought, it seeks eventually to bring them together.[28]

The virtue of eros is moderation. One of love's characteristic vices is to fail to combine properly, as with the ascetic or abstemious rejection of sensual pleasure, or to fail to combine properly by wallowing in me, you, or us—to ignore possible higher combinations. Its other characteristic vice is to try to merge or combine improperly, for example, to attempt an undifferentiated "combining" that does not allow separate independence or wholeness in its parts—mere licentiousness, say.

The virtue of spiritedness is courage, and its vices, as I indicated, are to be fearfully overcome and lose one's independence, to stiffen, repel, and overly isolate with excessive anger, or to lose independence in a risky and excessive attempt to unify. The virtues and vices of eros and spiritedness are also noticeable in the wholeness and identity they allow others.[29]

As movement, spiritedness separates me in my prideful identity. It also separates others and sees how they are separate but can then simply agglomerate them into my mastery, my city, my knowledge of unities. Spiritedness's separating and protecting may then also lead to protection of others' identity, as one protects a child or community as one's own. As movement, eros seeks first to join me with others in action or understanding but also sees me and them as perfect or perfectible combinations. Eros may then differentiate them, me, or us to the degree they are seen as sufficient and whole, even if they can then be further combined. Eros sees wonder, beauty, wholeness, and what attracts, and thumos sees perplexity, identity, possession, and what threatens.

To be free is to be open, to stand unhindered within a horizon of meaning, of goodness and intelligible order, and to gather and direct oneself within this, seeking and experiencing oneself and what is good. Erotic reaching out and admiring and spirited pushing away and enclosing, the first, basic, movements, are connected to freedom, which breaks and throws off chains, stands open, and directs or propels oneself. The dialectic subtlety in our movements and our poised openness for action and attempts to know go on to involve themselves in different stages and degrees of separating, differentiating, identifying, and combining. These are the first, most basic, workings of the soul—good things as completing and satisfactory (as beautifying) for us; justice as placing oneself in an ordered whole to experience what is noble; and "I" both as open to this and as bringing these things back to myself, to my own independence.

Liberal democratic freedom as the self-directed, increasingly unhindered movement to relieve unease, and the correlated experience of the self, is a version or deflection of this classical standpoint of the soul as seeking to be noble or whole. I will now explore liberal freedom by turning to the question of rights.

RIGHTS

We so closely connect freedom with rights in liberal democracies that we often call our rights our freedoms. What, then, is the natural basis of rights? Are they merely invented concepts, or are they actual properties? Let me first consider several current meanings. I have a right to be here: I've bought a ticket; I am a member of this class. I have just as much right to be here as anyone else. It's my right to say whatever I want or go wherever I wish. I have a right to use this land or mow this yard: I own it. I'm right (correct). I have the right to use this car: it is mine. These protections are my rights: the right to a speedy trial, the right to bear arms. The right to life, liberty, and the pursuit of happiness.

Looking at these uses, we see that rights involve permission, ownership, what is deserved, freedom, choice, and authority. The ticket or class membership gives me permission to sit in the theater or classroom; the rights to life, liberty, and property are their deserved use, direction, or ownership.

We may sum up these meanings and say that a right is a deserved authority, mastery, freedom, or choice. Central for us is the right to life, liberty, and the pursuit of happiness. One's right is one's own mastery or freedom—my own as differentiated from others, hence, fundamentally, my authority, what I master or dispose of. A right is an authority, ownership, mastery, or freedom to dispose of or to direct.

I have said that all attempts to clarify concepts have a context implicitly in mind from which we take our examples and from which we draw the concept's initial intelligibility. In the contemporary view of rights at play in my examples, the correlate is goods that are coherent with the equal rights of others. The ticket, weapon, trial, and use of land are, to begin with, equally available. This equal availability grounds believing that I have just as much right to be "here" as anyone else, or that I have the right to use this land: it was available, and I now own it; it is mine.

The goods over which one has authority are, for us, the basically interchangeable objects that can satisfy equal desires—those that from the public point of view we consider equal. The intellectual source of this view is Locke's understanding of pleasure as the relief from unease: the nature of desire is unease; such unease has the same quality whatever phenomenon causes or relieves it; and pleasure means only this relief. So the first approach of goods for those who have equal rights is their availability as what relieves unease or is a means to this.[30]

AUTHORITY

Rights are deserved authorities. What is "authority"? An authority is the one listened to or obeyed—the master, director, and, perhaps, originator or creator. Parents, priests, government, and (for their characters) the authors of dramas or novels are authorities. Authorities may be obeyed implicitly, but obedience is also often secured by punishment and threat.

My right is my authority. I am the one who freely directs, masters, leads, or guides myself. Such individual authority is naturally unavoidable, however restricted. External authorities may for a time be prominent, or punishment for disobeying them may be effective, but one can also stop listening to them. And as individual rights become the most significant authorities from the eighteenth century on, implicit obedience to other authorities, to priests, say, is reduced.[31] Government's authority, too, must then be traced back to individual authority, and in this fundamental sense it is restricted. Obeying or following others becomes at root voluntary, and, in time, the implicit authorities that remain powerful in countries that base themselves on natural individual authority weaken. This weakening is a prominent feature of the rapid change in expectations we see in our current culture.[32]

Individual authority is not the only natural authority. Parental authority is natural, to a point, and it is also the chief but increasingly remote natural ground of our weakening "traditional" authorities of religion, class, and occupation. Its ground is care, attention, love of one's own, and, for a while, greater knowledge and experience. Indeed, knowledge's right to guide is also natural. But knowledge must always justify itself by, ultimately, being able to make itself evident. It is not as such implicit, and it does not wield the power of punishment. It is not authoritative in these ways. How such knowledge makes its way politically and how it and false claims to it are properly limited is a significant political question. Prudence, let alone philosophical understanding, is difficult to recognize and must even sometimes hide itself. In our regime based on consent, knowledge and expertise can justly exercise direction only if those who would be directed voluntarily choose or permit this. This means that the unwise direct the wise—

but it also means that they can limit the sway of those who pretend to have expertise.

The grounds for mitigating this difficult practical problem of the relation of the wise and the unwise can be found in the fact that although few have expert knowledge of ways and means, many have sufficient understanding of the goals—health, prosperity, safety, legal justice—that guide the experts. Indeed, the ordinary grasp of these goals may be superior to experts' opinions.[33] Moreover, the virtue, the character, that is connected to prudence may be more visible than this prudence itself.[34] This will help us to choose the prudent to direct or represent us.

Legitimacy

Justified political rule is based on naturally justified authority. For political rule is justified as something chosen by free individuals, as an exercise of prudence that is connected to properly using and producing the community's goods, or as a kind of paternal concern.[35]

Justified rule is sometimes also called legitimate rule. The difference is that legitimacy focuses on the origin of the rulers rather than on their using their control properly.[36] Legitimate births and lines of succession are crucial in monarchies, especially when they serve, paternally, as it were, pious, holy, proper, and traditional ways, manners, and procedures. In regimes based on natural rights it is crucial to be able to trace a government to selection by the individual authorities, the voters, through proper procedure. Although the goal of good liberal government is to serve the people well by securing their rights and advancing the economic growth central for this, a government's legitimacy is based on origin, not success. Legitimate government can be a source of stability, but it does not guarantee, and may indeed work against, just and intelligent government.

Rights and Equality

My rights are my deserved authorities. What is their source? In the theory of equal rights and the political understanding built on it, my rights rest on the inescapable fact that I can reflect, choose, prefer, and act: I have self-movement or self-direction. This inescapable fact can be covered over or narrowed. But, once observed, once one sees oneself this way, one also sees no reasonable grounds to deny that this self-direction equally characterizes others. This is not to say that rights are exercised with equal wisdom or purity or that one actually allows others to enjoy them.

This existence of rights was first developed politically by considering one's own self-reflection and choice as they are linked to goods understood as satisfying desires, because it is such goods that are most clearly equal. They are also most visibly separable from the mass spirituality and otherworldliness against which modern thinkers rebelled.[37] They fit with seeing each of us as "subjects" who seek certainty for our own existence and who grasp what is satisfying as objects that are measured not independently but in terms of my own needs and desires. Securing equal individual rights as the heart of justice is coordinate with understanding goodness as what relieves unease.

Individual rights are individual authorities as opposed to common or priestly ones. They are not granted by others; rather, we can notice them as already there. No common rights, group rights, or class rights have the same immediate, inescapable, visibility and authority. Rights are the authority and self-direction that are one's own, one's inescapable property. But they require common effort to be secured.

This notion of rights becomes the ground of liberal democratic freedoms of speech, religion, and political consent but also of excessive claims about rights that in recent years forget their root in liberal democratic understanding. This notion also becomes the source of the view of rights we see in Kant and Hegel. In Kant, the will is free only by morally choosing or, indeed, intending to choose morally. Freedom is separated from natural choice or the natural "will" governed by desire, although it is coherent with equal rights. In Hegel, the seeming independence of individual rights is unstable apart from what rights reach toward. Developing this connection leads to and shows them to belong to a version of Kant's free will. This will, however, cannot itself ultimately be separated from fully reasonable political authority because to be fully, reasonably, defensible, morality must go beyond intention and be able to shape institutions and choices, not merely restrict or permit them.[38]

Kant's view grounds the notion that rights are (and must be) defensible apart from necessity and satisfaction, that they are "deontological," not protected by and subject to calculations of happiness. In the American world of John Locke as well, rights began as and remain a bulwark against attacks on the individual in the name of some "greater" additive or group happiness. Ultimately, rights are not found in a mysterious world of freedom separated from ordinary human motives and facts, or in mere calculation, but, rather, in the truth of human self-direction and inviolability.

RIGHTS AND SELF-MOVEMENT

Individual rights interpret the original phenomena from which they arise. These phenomena are visible not only in Hobbes and Locke and after them, but before. We can see this if we attend to my recent discussion of spiritedness and now consider more directly the gathered separateness of individuality. Indeed, it is precisely the experience of separateness, of one's separate unity, that is often insufficiently explored. This experience, as I have claimed, is the heart of warding off attacks, of bringing things back to oneself and one's own, of incorporating and possessing, of mastery, of risk, of stubbornness. This separation does not simply nullify the world or others, the outside. It separates from, holds off, looks at, and brings back or incorporates.

We can interpret the experience of separateness and self-direction in several ways. Once we isolate and discuss the experience we tend to repeat or develop one of these ways because we cannot fully divide our experience from our understanding.

As I have indicated, the first and most basic articulated interpretation of this experience is the classical notion of thumos, most familiar as the soul's second part as Plato describes it in the *Republic*. We can see it, too, as the seat of the virtues of courage, proper anger, and pride. This experience is also the chief origin of the separate movement and authority that, together with reflection and choice, define rights. For the classics, the development of spiritedness to full pride tends to try to incorporate all to oneself, to one's honor alone. In Nietzsche's view of the priority of will to power, to offer a second example, the superman acts as if he forms, orders, or commands all, as if he brings it all into being, as if he can re-create all that has been produced historically.[39] With liberal rights, our independence is correlated with securing or ascertaining oneself fully and to understanding goods as what relieves unease. My unity is correlated not with classic nobility or honor but with desire and security and with what is, therefore, a more equal self-assertion than we see with the classics. The classical soul that connects eros and thumos involves a pride and nobility that go beyond the self-certain separateness of the modern I, and a satisfaction more complete than modern pleasure and desire. My powers are oriented to what is good, useful, and beautiful, which one observes and with which one combines; everything outside is not simply fodder for one's security or command.

ONE'S OWN

The central experience from which rights emerge is the experience of one's separateness and unity. Can we say more about this experience of one's own, oriented to the question of rights? One's own is not simply the body, as is sometimes said, because one's own is experienced even in the most bodiless encounters. Being lost in thought, in thought about what is general, even in identical mathematical thoughts with others, is still my being lost in thought. I experience general thoughts as mine. What defines my own is also not (self-)"consciousness," because what is in question is the "my," the experience of "my," the intelligibility or meaningfulness of "my" in my consciousness, or the "self" in self-consciousness if one talks of self-consciousness.[40] Rather, my own is first or primarily the experience of the movement of separation that freely directs the things and powers one masters or controls.

Nonetheless, one's separateness in the classical sense cannot as experienced or even in discussion be distinguished altogether from eros, because I am both. One also experiences an opening toward, a reaching out in order to combine, and not only a separating or distinguishing from, because "I" cannot preserve or understand myself simply as separate or unconnected. I am always involved in some immersion and in a moving out that is also a taking back.[41] Still, when one considers rights one first sees the separated, enclosing "I" that takes back, the assertion of security, because this is more literally distinctive in "I," one's own, prior even to dealing with one's articulated self.

The separating involved in any understanding of "I," and, therefore, of rights, is an experienced movement of pushing away from or enclosing and absorbing. This movement is in terms of something concrete, but, at the same time, as I have said, it is in terms of the context in which what is concrete emerges or to which it belongs. How "I" see myself, the "just" whole or way to which I belong and from which I separate, and how goods first approach as good are correlated. These are not external causes but belong to the very experience and grasp of things.

I have argued that the usual ordinary contexts in which I am immersed press outward to the usual broadest context, the way of life as organized in the political community. The ordinary contexts are formed by an implicit and sometimes explicit understanding of the way that goods guide us and fit together. But our individual choices and activities can also be separated from the full control of our city and regime even if we do not recognize this explicitly, because our regime belongs to this still broader understanding of what is good and just and is therefore questionable or incomplete. So any activity that attracts me has a certain independence.

The understanding of separateness and individuality within which one's self resides belongs to this complexity. Spiritedness is the ground of this understanding, but how far separateness is developed differs in different regimes. As with the goods we enjoy, this separation is greater some places than others. The understanding of goodness and of the organization and (in)equality of parts within a regime also varies with regimes.

The different ways we can understand and ground our separateness, and the different orders of justice, fit, and goodness to which "I" may belong, mean that rights truly exist but are not the whole truth. "Rights" interpret our individuality or identity, our self-movement and self-authority, our spiritedness, in a vital way, once we liberate ourselves from obfuscation. But it is an average, universal, or equal way, not one oriented to nobility or to command. Rights are an interpretation of the self-ownership and the stiffness, stubbornness, and recalcitrance (pride) that always ground objection to (one's own) slavery, even in regimes that justify slavery. They belong to a context that organizes and distributes goods and opportunities for the purpose of securing equal authority and, thus, equal consent. This liberal interpretation of spiritedness also connects the self to goods and pleasures that it is difficult to doubt. In this sense, "I" in a liberal democracy replaces priestly authority with equal individual authority.

RIGHTS, REVERENCE, AND INVIOLABILITY

Individual rights also speak to reverence for the individual. This experience grounds justifying (a degree of) equal authority. Such reverence is the experience of attention to what is high in oneself, what gives one pause in dealing with oneself, in relation to goods and what is high in them. It belongs to our possibility of directing ourselves to what guides us correctly or uplifts us and sustaining ourselves in this. Rights interpret this reverence in a certain way—in an egalitarian way with egalitarian goods.

The height connected to reverence speaks to the role of reason in directing our powers. All our passions are intellectual or "noetic" in the sense that we experience them together with reason, with combining, separating, and directing. This is why opinion is important in experiencing justice, goodness, and virtue and is a ground of our ability to question and compare different ways. But some passions are more clearly or exclusively noetic than others because they are not, or not primarily, felt physically, or because as feelings they are not directed to or grounded on what is physical. Laughter at pretense, for example, is based on the difference between nature and convention. Reverence is based on and points to one's true height and separateness. It is the twin of laughter and sometimes laughter's ("irreverence's") seeming opposite.[42] Perplexity, another noetic feeling, is directed to instability, unclarity, questionability, and being enclosed; and experiencing wonder, attraction to the wonderful, is ultimately directed to the self-sufficient, outstanding, and complete.[43]

Reverence belongs to the noetic passions. Reverence is for the high and guiding. It is also, and perhaps especially, for what should not be desecrated or ridiculed, in all things but primarily for the high and guiding as such, which other things reflect. It is for the pure. Reverence is or can be coherent with the experience of one's protectedness, one's pride, not merely in order to remain alive or to incorporate property as one's own, but as someone who should live up to his high possibilities. Rights belong to the experience of honoring oneself, one's separateness as deserving honor. So rights, as individual authority, combine one's spirited separateness as the one who asserts, wills, and chooses with the erotic movement toward excellence or perfection. Rights are this inviolability, this inviolable authority, interpreted as equal and therefore universal; and because the goods one deals with outside oneself are, through rights, largely reduced to pleasure, it is primarily the selves who are honored.[44]

Rights as one's own authority connect a kind of spirited separateness and reverence. Reverence generally, of course, is also related to the gods, the holy understood as what guides us and frames our world, or suffuses or penetrates things with a kind of purity. It is especially this element of good things—purity—that is key in reverence and to a degree in self-reverence, and in the beloved as perfect. It is echoed in the inviolability, the deserved authority, that characterizes rights.

Is such an experience of one's independence as pure a necessary or inevitable experience? The holy things are not simply to be used. How do they differ from the beautiful and noble, also not simply to be used?[45] The religious experience of holiness differs from eros. As with eros, it is connected to admiration. But there is also often an element of awe and fear in it: holy things have powers beyond ours that are more pure than we can be but also, perhaps, can instigate terror. The religious experience of the holy is the experience of the pure, upward-compelling, honorable, magisterial, awesome, and un-avoidable, what is not to be (or gods not capable of being) merely used or misused. But the element of fear of holy gods as opposed to awe as wonder (which lacks fear) or of the magisterial as frightening rather than simply wonderful or grand is (or can be made) secondary in proper natural reverence, and perhaps even a distortion of it. Innocent (pure) children, or oneself as inviolable and pure, center on the beau-tiful, wonderful, and good; the holy is the element of purity in the wonderful or beautiful.

The natural element of fearful activity related to holy things comes from protecting the inviolable against others and against mere interests—the spirited element in security and government's punish-ing laws and, beyond nature, punishing gods. The "holy" is what one protects in its beauty, purity, separateness, nobility, and wonder rather than simply possessing it, and this protection is then also compatible with knowing and admiring it, which is erotic. The holy and inviolable in oneself are an echo of this. In rights, self-inviolability emphasizes security of self because we hold ourselves to be equal, and goods are what help to relieve unease. The liberal virtues protect and secure rights, as does the regime, more than these virtues belong to enjoying the fully excellent or pleasant. Our rights are our separate authorities to choose, our prideful or responsible authority and authoritative or responsible pride.

The experience of oneself as subject to, or standing within, the natural in its beauty, attraction, and purity is a central element in the experience connected to rights. Rights, however, are a narrow and equal version of this, oriented to security. They are the experience of oneself as separate, unavoidable, self-protecting, authoritative, in-violable, and not simply to be used. But it is also true that, given the dominance of securing equal rights in liberal regimes, things outside the self tend to lose their own separate beauty and sanctity and are experienced initially and in time concretely merely as means to an end or as subject to mastery. One sees this in Locke's understanding of value as coming almost exclusively from human effort, not from nature, and in Hegel's understanding of property.[46]

THE ELEMENTS OF RIGHTS

There are, thus, three elements in instituting and securing rights. The first is the attempt to cut through priestly obfuscation, so that one's own authoritative self-direction and assertion is linked to what deserves to be revered rather than bowing down to priests as the only guardians of the pure. Pride or spiritedness belongs to one's own inviolability. The second is connecting rights to goods seen as meeting ordinary desires and producing ordinary pleasures, where these are reliefs from unease and unranked in their choiceworthiness. Such good things are first grasped in a way that ignores their independence. Hence they become objects of use, mastery, and exchange. But the inviolability of one's separate rights remains central. The third, as I will soon discuss, is virtue, in particular responsibility, understood as protecting rights. The coordinated elements of justice, good, and "I" make any one of these elements taken alone not fully explicable. Inviolability becomes connected to rights, to equally prideful self-assertion, only together with goods and virtues grasped in a certain way.

VIRTUE I

Let me restate and briefly develop several points of this discussion. Rights are meant to be secured; that is, individual authority is meant to be secured, equally. What is being secured is prideful or separated inviolability, held equally, and, therefore, in a limited way. The correlate to this in terms of the approach of goods as "good" is desire as unease and the relief of unease as pleasure, with no ranking as such of these goods. Material growth is required for this, to provide a sufficient degree and level of satisfaction and, therefore, security or certainty, and to allow the safe liberation of spirited ("entrepreneurial") talent and even the (partial) mastery, possession, or incorporation of (rather than openness toward) nature.[47] But for this way of life to prevail, a certain kind of character, a certain kind of virtue, is necessary, as well as a certain stance toward government—government based on equal authoritative election or consent; institutions formed as limited, separated, powers; and a constitution or whole that is something that we ourselves make and limit, hence something not revered as divine but as an element of self-reverence, reverence for us, for our way, for our founding fathers.[48]

A first statement about virtue is thus in order. Virtue specifies the character one needs—the human type one needs—fully to enjoy justice and goodness in a regime. In our case, virtue specifies the character I need to secure my rights. It is not enough to attempt to allow others to secure them for me, although one needs others, too, because one is not sufficiently free alone. The key modern virtue is responsibility. Responsibility is similar but not equal to the classics' great pride. Great pride is about honor, but it concerns my distinction beyond or above others, not equality, equal will, or equal authority, and it involves ranked pleasures that are connected to the correct sources and objects. So it is higher than responsibility but less equal, and the good with which it deals is not a momentary resting but a kind of burgeoning and expansiveness. (In liberal democracy a likeness to this can still in serious circumstances occur.) Moral dignity in the contemporary post-Kantian sense is also related to but differs from rights and responsibility. It is either too separated from seeking material things and actively using freedom—too merely moral to be the same as responsibility—or, as it sometimes is used, too much emphasizes the material trappings of independence rather than the right balance of property, opportunity, and rights.

The Self, Properly Understood

The discussion of rights and of their ground raises the question of the fullest, most adequate, presence and understanding of the separate self and inviolability, and the standards by which to judge the merit of different standpoints.

This judgment involves, first, bringing out the experience of separation, protection, incorporation, and self-reverence that would be oriented to what is most meaningful—to what most fully orients and guides. What enables this orientation would be correlated with the fullest individuality or identity. This unity would allow mastery, but as directedness toward what one is immersed within, and confident movement within it. It is, therefore, not limited to rights or to what one can produce almost ex nihilo in a Nietzschean manner. Second, this judgment involves understanding the full use of the powers seen in this separateness, oriented to one's way of life and, ultimately, to the true whole that any way of life, any order of justice, imitates. It involves, third, seeing what most fully allows the other elements in one's regime—the virtues and other ends and individuals—their natural independence. These are the criteria of guidance and choice that then allow comparison.

There is, however, no perfect consistency among these elements. These factors cannot be made simply coherent with each other because of the difficulty of each thing's (and each of us) showing its fullest power either alone or together with others. One cannot perfectly link one's own, our own, what is best, and what is most just. The highest possibility appears to be the philosophical life, with its full use of one's own powers, openness to the full whole, and experience of much, but not all, of the variety in ordinary experience. Full reflection allows the greatest understanding of separate parts, and wholes as wholes. Still, one can at best see partial truth but not the whole truth. Next would seem to be education to philosophy and education politically to what is good and just in statesmanship, and, then, statesmanship itself, because of the breadth and complexity of the questions with which statesmen deal.[49]

Chapter Three

The Nature of
Power and Property

Central to any political discussion is power. We also use "power," as I just did, to describe our abilities—our power to think, to write, to feel. Power and ability are often synonyms: my power to think is my ability to think. But they are not always synonyms: I may have powerful or weak emotions but not able ones. Power and ability, moreover, also sometimes call to mind what is potential as opposed to what is actual or necessary, although to be "potent" seems to be actually powerful.

My interest is in power both as and as differentiated from power as ability. What causes this interest is not only the importance of the phenomenon but also the variety in thinkers' understanding of it. It is basic intellectually for Aristotle and Plato, Hobbes and Locke, Heidegger and Nietzsche.[1] We also wonder whether different understandings exist in different ways of life, or, rather, whether we find the same understanding, with power merely held by different groups or people.

What Is Power?

We begin with our current uses. He has too much power. He has tyrannical power. He has a powerful hold on her. The country has great military and economic power. He is a powerful pianist. He plays the piano powerfully. He is awfully powerful. He has great intellectual power. His powers are failing. The real power is his wife. He is the power behind the throne. Who has the real power here? I'd like to help, but it's not in my power. Executive, legislative, and judicial power. Air power and sea power. He's lost the power to hear. This will be a powerful storm. He has a powerful right hand, left hook, serve. Human powers. That's a powerful sound. The roadrunner does not have the power to fly. He can see again; he has regained the power of sight. This crop has the power to feed millions. She has a powerful artistic imagination. He is a powerful man; you don't want to cross him, you can't move him. The powers that be. A powerful sight, story, piece of music. Powerful features, odors, tastes. Powerful emotions, loves, attachments.

If we gather these uses, what common meanings do we find? Power is strength or force—the powerful tennis serve or left hook. But it is not only general force: the powerful serve can belong together with a weak backhand, or powerful driving with weak putting. Power is force in a specific area. But what is force here? It is connected to movement: speed and distance, quick speed and long distance. But it is also connected to accuracy: the powerful backhand is an accurate one, difficult to return and unfailing, not merely quick. "Powerful" is both forceful and strong—the fast serve or long drive—and accurate or good: both together, where relevant.

Power as strength can also harm or destroy: military strength, the powerful left hook, the powerful serve or drive that hits someone, the powerful patron one should not annoy, the powers that be, the powerful storm. A powerful force (often) destroys even when it accomplishes: the powerful jackhammer or crane. Yet it does not only destroy: the powerful lift or crane can both assemble and disassemble, military power can conquer but for good purposes (although the purpose is in a way external to the power, it seems). Military power as strength can also ward off or defend. The economically powerful man can prevent harmful things from occurring.

If we summarize our analysis (to this point) of power as strength we should say that it involves speed and force—movement—that tends to destroy or break up (separate). But it may also hold fast against destruction and may then reassemble or put together. For power as strength can hold firm against attempts to move one or to break things apart and separate them: it is to be recalcitrant or stubborn. And strength can be for a further purpose of putting together or building, as one (or a machine) has strength to set materials in place. In sum, power as strength is movement that primarily breaks up, separates, destroys, or thwarts this, even if this strength is ultimately for integrating or combining. Someone powerful makes things happen, shakes things up, changes them, or prevents this.

We also speak of power where it means strength in another way. The powerful storm destroys. But what of powerful odors or tastes, which we also call strong odors or tastes? What of strong or powerful vision, or a powerful vision of a better world? We speak of powerful sounds, and sometimes of strong ones by which we primarily mean loud or resonant ones. Indeed, we also speak of powerful sights. We also sometimes speak of having a powerful feel for a situation and often of a strong or powerful grip on things.

These are examples of power as strength, although, as we will see, they are also connected to power as ability. But what does strength as power mean here? The powerful or strong odor or taste is a large amount of its type. But a large amount can be scattered, and what is scattered or dissipated is not powerful. The powerful or strong taste or odor is concentrated, brought together, and verges on excess or is indeed an excess (measured in relation to a task or to other things happening in the usual environment). It is a concentration of the element sensed. But sensed elements—say, sensed sounds or odors—belong to something. They are loud songs or bells. The strong odor is the smell of an onion, say, even if not identified immediately.

Strength as concentration or intensity, therefore, is another element of power. What is concentrated has a powerful presence, as I said: it is not scattered. It is prominent: it does not recede. Indeed, we speak of powerful or strong features—those that are prominent, visible, and stand out. What is powerful stands out, catches one's attention, or distinguishes. One feature of the powerful as strong, therefore, is to be concentrated or prominent.

We can say still more about the meaning of power as strength. For we talk of powerful emotions, loves, hates, ideas, or of someone who makes a powerful impression. To what meaning does this point? When we talk of powerful emotions we also say strong ones. Strength, again, is a central meaning of power.

What element of strength do we have in mind here? "Emotions" indicate that the power is one of movement. One can also see this from our descriptions of emotions and from the term itself: shuddering or recoiling in fear; being attracted or compelled "magnetically"; a powerful, "mesmerizing" (freezing), "magical" (transporting) performance—a riveting or enchanting one where one is transported beyond, floats beyond, oneself.[2] A powerful idea is (among other things) one that generates other ideas or fills one's understanding. A strong passion or emotion suffuses or overwhelms everything, so that there is no room for other passions. Everything is colored from its point of view.

Power here is strength of motion and expansion. What is the specific strength that is involved? One is concentration or intensity, the totality and comprehensiveness that suffuses. Another is channeling, directing, making it difficult to move or work in another direction. The fixing or fixation is the way that the powerful fills the available "space."[3]

So to be powerful (as being strong) is to be concentrated (intense), prominent (present, outstanding, overwhelming, a suffusing singularity), and to move (attract, repel, discombobulate, rivet, transport, divert), primarily as pulling or breaking apart (separating) or keeping apart (protecting) but sometimes also to bring recalcitrant parts together. Strength is a concentrated gathering for movement, including fixing in place. The one who is powerful moves others, often but not only against their natural inclination. This is especially the case when strength is forceful separation.[4]

ABILITY

The second significant meaning of power, the second phenomenon to which it points, is ability. We speak of the human power to speak, or of human powers generally. These powers can be strong or weak (powerful or not), so they are not identical to strength. We speak of a bird's or an airplane's power of flight or of a powerful pianist, one with significant ability whose playing might be gentle, not strong. We speak of the power of hearing and sight or of someone's powerful artistic imagination. In all these cases power means ability (and with some of our examples, strength, too.) But what is an ability? Is it a possibility, such as a coiled snake, or an activity, something actual? One could hardly recognize abilities without seeing them used, employed, active. But a power is not exhausted in its present and past activities or in any set of activities (unless it disappears through these activities as do insects that mate once and die). Still the range of its possibilities may already be evident from its present instances. What more, for example, can we say about birds' flight, once we have seen them fly? Yet it may be that a bird or plant has more powers than we now know, or abilities seen or stated more fully in new situations. Plants can show new medicinal powers, for example, or we can study hummingbirds to see exactly how they hover. Powers are abilities that are also possibilities or potentials, because powers are not all exhausted by what one is doing or has done.[5]

What more can we say about ability or potential? Here we are likely to think that each ability varies concretely, so that anything that we say generally about "ability" misses the point. What does a bird's ability to fly have in common with a man's ability to speak?

What one can say generally is that abilities allow a thing to be what it is or constitute what it is. This normally means that something's abilities show what it does, as birds fly, but also what can be done with it, what the thing allows or even tends to encourage you to do with or to it—sit on it, write with it, hammer with it.

So a power is an ability to do, affect, or be affected. It is what something is in terms of what it does or affects, often when this ability (or abilities) chiefly characterizes what the thing is. Someone's powers of thinking or performing are diminishing, we might say; that is, his abilities to make his way around his (or all humans') specific area or environment are diminishing. Powers as abilities are that by which something does what it does (or allows what it allows), where this doing or acting means making its way around its defining context successfully—flying, thinking, composing, fighting.

Let me now return to strength to reach a combined or more complete understanding. As I said, strength is a concentrated gathering for movement, speed, destruction, and suffusing or overwhelming. The gathering is a pulling together and in and, therefore, also a separating from others. It is the concentration of abilities on or toward something. In "strength," abilities primarily separate, destroy, or protect from this, often against the immediate natural inclination of the thing forced.

Something's abilities are concentrated gatherings for moving or affecting. Not all ability, however, is the kind of strength used primarily to disperse or separate, or to prevent this. Things' powers are concentrated gatherings in relation to their task and environment. This may mean gentle movement or dispersal, not forceful movement, or combining, not separating. What is concentrated in order to affect or be affected may bring together and not only disperse. How full the gathering of something's ability is, moreover, is a central measure of its excellence, although not the only one. This excellence also depends on the ability's success. Moreover, to judge excellence we also need to know how complete the work itself is for which abilities are used and in which they are embedded—how beautiful, pleasant, and choice-worthy the task, or that for which it is ministerial or functional. Is the house that a builder constructs with powerful instruments beautiful or merely useful, is it a criminal's house, is the cleverly designed powerful weapon used by a tyrant, or to defend freedom, and so on?

POWER AND WHAT THINGS ARE

I will turn now to how ability helps us understand what makes something what it is by differentiating it from other things—by, along with its shape (often connected to its powers), providing what distinguishes it, its boundaries or limit. If we try to differentiate men and birds, for example, we point first to each one's look and shape. But we also consider the thing's look when it is in motion, in action. And this involves its powers. We refine our views of these powers with learning and observation, moreover, so that, say, the different shapes, sizes, and modes of flight differentiate butterflies from birds. Not only the shape, but the visible or prominent power—here, flight—is a major, or the central, differentiating element. This is especially true of what is not altogether perceptible—reason and the proper or virtuous directing of passions, for example.

I also mean here to consider the connections among powers and purposes as well as shapes. Something's power answers the questions, what does it do, what can it do, what is it able to do? Its look or shape and, where relevant, its purpose are connected but not identical to this. The more independent something can be—the bird, for example—the more we can say about the thing and its powers as it stands on its own. Otherwise, when we consider something (say, a nail) we also implicitly have in mind its broader functions or purposes, its context of activities. The more a thing can organize different materials, moreover—say, courage as dealing with fear in battle but also as dealing with other fears and risks—the more we can learn about its full powers. The more something stands on its own (is independent) and orders or contains a variety of materials and aspects in a variety of regimes, the more it "is" when to be is to be powerful and independent.[6]

Let me briefly discuss this in light of human powers. Our look or obvious shape is central in distinguishing us. So, too, is the range and panoply of our activities, and our independence. So, too, is our distinctive power of speech and the separations and combinations it sees, and how it brings out, forms, and governs our other powers—our passions, say, and their subsequent effect. Our abilities correlate to and enable us to make our way around the central realms in which we live and act, the areas that we carry with us, as it were. Given this, for humans, speech or reason is central. Our powers, moreover, are not efficient causes but, rather, the defining elements in what we do, especially once we see this in the light of our perfections. The perfections of our powers show their full capability.

I have made various points about our fullest powers or the fullest use of our distinctive abilities. Not all our abilities are distinctive, nor does each of us have the full measure of them.[7] Still, our distinctive human abilities allow the most scope, given the right circumstances, to all our other abilities: they should rule or direct these other abilities. Properly or reasonably directed emotion, or properly directed physical force, will allow these capacities sufficient reign but not allow them to rule completely.

PROPER GUIDANCE

To bring out still more fully issues of proper direction or guidance I will again discuss power as strength. We sometimes consider strength or force to be overbearing and misused: power often suggests an excessive, unlimited, domineering, or tyrannical use of force. The powerful man makes others dance to his tune. This power does not merely mean separating or rearranging two things stuck together or sending a ball flying, but, rather, it is separating someone from his possessions, destroying what he owns, or forcing him to engage in untoward activities for the powerful man's own ends or pleasure.[8] This is power as strength or force, especially where force allows control. To control means to move something or keep it moving against its own (immediate) inclination (even if it is a step toward its fuller inclination). It is to move the thing or person as one wishes, to separate or alienate something from itself, as it were.[9] To use power or strength can be to separate things from themselves, to move them against their own tendency, or to keep them from moving according to their tendency, to cage the bird or prisoner, to forbid the desired activity, to stop the advance or advancer. (Hence, others' force opposes my freedom.) Power is in this case the concentration of someone's or something's abilities in order to separate things from themselves, to direct them against their natural or desired course or inclination.[10] At first blush, this power can be for good or ill, but when we think of power as sheer force or sheer strength or as excessive or misused it is this harmful or unnatural element that comes to light. Proper power is measured concentration on proper tasks or movements that allows one and others to follow their natural inclinations and, consequently, sometimes to improve their immediate inclinations.[11] To improve means to liberate their fuller inclinations as one does while educating children and students, teaching, tending gardens, and perhaps even training animals or using "resources" that keeps their form but concentrates some of their inclinations.

What also comes to light in power as improper force is destroying something's form or independence, controlling and misdirecting not only its own abilities and inclinations, but its unity itself. Power or mastery over nature, for example, may take something's powers or capacities, what it is capable of, and concentrate or focus on one or two of these such that their inclinations on their own are so ignored or misdirected that the distinctive thing in its form is overlooked or destroyed.[12] Strength (or force) as this kind of separating or rearranging is an element of power.

POWER AND POLITICAL PHILOSOPHERS

Let me advance the discussion by considering three thinkers and the result of their thought. In Hobbes and Locke, power appears to have a more expansive meaning than I have discussed. This is so in one respect; in another respect it is narrower. For Hobbes, power is any means to secure one's ends, one's ends are the satisfaction of desire, all desires are equal because "good" is what someone desires (not what attracts independently or intrinsically), desire is (as with Locke but less clearly) relief from unease, political power originates in individual power or authority, and politics (again, more clearly in Locke) largely involves arranging institutional means or "powers," for example, by separating them. A "power," thus, is not the particular ability of a particular kind of thing, as is the human power of speech. It is not an "ability" as what allows something to make its way around its defining area. And it is not the activity of what forms or organizes. Rather, a power is a means to what helps relieve unease or satisfy desire. Hobbes therefore can say that we seek power after power until death. And Locke can make a central chapter of his *Essay Concerning Human Understanding* a chapter on "power" in which he discusses liberty and being directed by the strongest desire.

This split of power from specific abilities connected to specific forms, areas, and completions allows power to mean anything that can have any effect. What the dividing of power from things' specific abilities also does is to allow to come to the fore the element of strength (or force) that consists in moving things away from their natural inclination and separating and putting them together as one chooses. It also splits strength from specific things and areas—tennis rackets and the balls they hit, music and emotion, even strong smells— and sees physical strength as merely one version of strength. Power is the manipulation (the control) of any motion or of things in motion, as one sees fit. Not the end or forming but simply the moving is key. And what one sees fit to do is to satisfy one's own most general motions or desires. The free self, moreover, the self of self-movement or mastery, the self to be secured or preserved (through power) in this mastery, is the calculating self that is liberated (or seeking to be liberated) for continued independent self-motion from all claims that are not authoritatively self-chosen. All goods and actions tend to be seen in this light. (The limit to one's individual mastery is the equal rights of others, which results in competition, and government.)

Modern and Classical Democracy

Is such a liberal self, and power and motion so understood, a classical possibility that merely happens to be developed after the advent of Christianity, or is it something fundamentally new? From a political standpoint, the equality of selves and citizens based on natural rights is both like and unlike classical democracy, like it because based on equality and liberty but unlike it because liberal democracy comes to be considered the best form of government rather than an acceptable but inferior one.[13] It is also unlike classical democracy because of its greater denigration of pride, honor, and nobility, the reduction of full virtue, the justification of the utility and not only beauty of scientific knowledge, the abolition of slavery, the civic equality of women, the favoring of economic expansion, the narrowing and equalizing of pleasure, the permitting of toleration, the (relative) separation of the private from the public, the existence of representation, and, starting with Locke's separation of powers, the utility of internal clash or dissent within government. What is equal in the free self and its objects replaces the nobility to which classical freedom tends, and which is therefore echoed in classical democracy.

How different in fact, however, is the way of life of classical and modern democracy? In both there is virtue, (some) freedom, religion, art, and thought. Technological plenty leads to greater health, comfort, and equality in modern life, but the elements of such health and comfort are not novel. Virtue is narrowed, but it is also expanded. Consider, for example, the continued relevance of Aristotle's virtues today and, also, the new or revised modern virtues such as responsibility. Intellectual life and popular art seem to be flattened today, but is this flattening in fact true of all our music, painting, and literature?

It would appear, then, that we can judge the differences between classical democracy and our liberal democracy in common terms but without numerical commensurability by which one could weigh exactly what has been gained and lost in human virtue, and without numerical commensurability that would allow one to calculate the merits of the spread of individual freedom as distinguished from its excellent use.

Perhaps, however, there are matters that we cannot compare in the experience of classical and modern (democratic) activities, which, in turn, would restrict their commensurability altogether and not only lead to factually different rankings: perhaps there are experiences in modern democracy that are simply new. What, however, could these be? Is it, then, easier to say that the experience of all things classical changes in modernity because of their different grounding in modernity, leading classical and modern democracy to be wholly incommensurable? If all movement and ability in modern liberalism is fungible as "power," and all limits can be overcome through force (strength), how could the liberal experience of virtue, the beautiful, thought, and love remain the same as it is with the classics, except, largely, verbally. If "I" am a free subject who masters or self-directs in this unitary way, and what "satisfies" is only what is for myself and my security with no independent excellence in things, what common ground could there be with classical nobility? "Metaphysical" or "ontological" elements such as power and satisfaction enter the very basis of our experiences, which experiences, therefore, would not be comparable in the ancient and modern world.

We could say, in reply, however, that much political and metaphysical comparability would exist at the beginning of the shift from the classical to the modern and, then, step by step away from the classics. Perhaps comparison rests on backward reference through a historical path. Yet, we might reply, there is no valid comparison from where we are today, where we have now ended. But why? If at the beginning, why not still? Indeed, it is perhaps our engaging in common historical discussion that is central, as if one were newly creating or discovering and thus comparing each step from the classics to the moderns and on.[14] One takes the point of view of each major discoverer or creator, then of his audience. This is especially useful when one looks at political-moral ways of life, and at what is transformed there. But it is also true metaphysically. Nonetheless, if experience is always noetic and understanding changes, so, too, must experience. But perhaps "new" understanding and, thus, experience is always a variant or possibility of what is first, and what is first is fullest and broadest, and is the ground of proper experience and understanding of the just, virtuous, beautiful, free, powerful, and so on. At the least, one begins with the classics, or works one's way back to them so that one can begin with them, in order to arrive at the root experiences that are the clue to the fullest experience. The fact that we can start with today's meanings and see so much about the basic phenomena shows something about where we are now, and about continuity. The experiences are different but less so than one is taught to believe. The modern view of power and democracy differs from but can be likened to and judged by the classical view.

NIETZSCHE

Another fundamental discussion of power is in Nietzsche, who understands power to be the essence of all things. To be powerful is to be commanding and organizing. It is not commanding for a purpose but is the discharge of what commands, what rules, what is above or on top. Each other thing is organized to enhance the discharge of what commands. Everything fights to command, to express itself truly.[15]

From this point of view, separate abilities and forms are no longer defining. Rather, amount and calculation are vital, as with Hobbes and Locke, but not as means to satisfy desires. Greater or stronger power is what moves, places and replaces, separates and combines (organizes), but not in a way that allows the parts to be independent or sees and brings out their independent ability.[16] Even what Nietzsche clarifies as the unconscious is humanized by our power, by being brought into a mastery of drives, knowingly or consciously. Power is creating, not as making new products, but as ordering and reordering for discharge and treating as fully one's own creation what has been fated for one historically. As with other significant thinkers, Nietzsche takes an element common in all understanding—drives as strength—and makes it paramount but, then, also transforms our understanding of wholes, ends, freedom, the "I," justice, and other metaphysical elements in his new light.

USING POWER

A central issue, of course, is how to use power properly. This issue begins with the question of the degree to which the presence of power, as strength, already includes or points to its proper use. To say the least, this cannot clearly be so, because of power's obvious misuse. Yet it is also true that force, if attained according to some justification, is limited by the way of life or whole to which it belongs. Strength exercised under law is always somewhat restricted, as strength in a specific area is limited by the rules under which it is exercised (the tennis serve or golf drive) or the boundaries of what it concentrates (odors, sounds, etc.). Where it seems least self-limiting is where a "strongman" is unchained by law or institutions, operates in a sphere with no rivals, or uses strength for purposes that seem to lack their own natural limits, as is true of unlimited pleasure as the goal of Plato's tyrants.[17]

Claiming that power points to its proper use seems especially Pollyannaish when legal limits have little effect or still allow massive destruction, as with the Nazis and the USSR. The more that power is merely a means stripped from any goals, the more remote are its limits, and the more one needs to take explicit action against its excess. Nonetheless, even strength without purpose or simply as willful destruction faces some restrictions—the reaction that comes from subverting trust or ordinary goals politically, or the limits inherent in the narrow satisfaction of willful rearranging and destroying. Indeed, a related limit comes from experiencing the pointlessness or insufficient satisfaction that derives from the mere accumulation of power or adulation (if this is the goal). Strength apparently without purpose is often in fact directed and limited by the desires one chooses to satisfy or the unease one seeks to relieve: the accumulation of strength is still experienced together with these limits. To say that proper use is endemic to an activity or, at least, that excess is unsatisfying, however, is not to say that these limits are sufficiently self-exercising. But there will be an objective narrowing of the soul of the misusing strongman, if not always clearly felt.

Using Abilities

We can speak more confidently of experienced limits when we think of power as ability. The question, again, is whether the experience of our powers, our abilities, already involves an experience of their proper use. In general, it does to the degree that opinion and understanding belong to the experience and are implicated in connecting it to and separating it from others.

One clue to this is when we call someone able or very able. To be very able is to have a great deal of ability, and this points to excellent use. The clearest example is speech or reason itself, where using it to describe, point out, compare, deduce, and so on carries with it an understanding of imperfection and, therefore, of perfection: of being inexact or imprecise, of not saying all there is to say, of different grounds of comparison, and of continued unseen or unexplored deductive possibilities. An imprecise activity is experienced in its imprecision as well as in its relative accuracy, and it therefore points to greater precision. This orientation to excellence is so not merely of efforts to say what is true, moreover, but is also visible as speech that commands, that is playful or comic, that evokes tears or smiles, that persuades and cajoles, that defends and wards off. These, too, speak to or from something that is true: a laughable discrepancy, an expected reward or threat, an authoritative difference, genuine sympathy. Such speech, in its speaking and its continued reconsidering, has an internal experience and standard of best and better. So one can strive to be more effective, persuasive, amusing, or commanding. With greater or lesser awareness one notices why what succeeded did, and how to improve the ability's exercise.[18]

Virtue II

The question now is whether this orientation to proper use is also true of our other distinctive powers. We can say at once that it is so at least to the degree that they involve speech, given what I have just claimed. Aristotle's *Ethics* considers twelve ethical virtues. In each, one deals with the passion or good in question in a measured way: one seeks, enjoys, or deals with it in the right way, at the right time, for the right reason, with the right people, as measured by practical reason. Our virtuous choices and actions involve measured thought and, therefore, point to properly measured thought. It is possible once or twice to imitate a virtuous choice cleverly or dishonestly. But this can continue only in the unlikely event that one's habits are completely unformed by constant proper action. Even occasional fraud, moreover, is limited if law also commands what is proper.

But does proper measure affect the very experience of the passions, pleasures, and goods? Do these experiences point to virtuous enjoyment? Consider the proper experience of beautiful things and dealing with them. Because beauty is a compound of what stands out on its own, is fitting, and is attractive, to experience things in their beauty involves measured enjoyment from the beginning. This is less obvious but still true of the experience of useful goods such as wealth, where the attraction of the good, how it presents itself as choiceworthy, belongs together implicitly or explicitly with some measure both of its independent desirability and of its place in a more or less just whole. This measure directs what one pursues for one's own enjoyment or the goods that one generously gives away. Virtue is happiness because it enjoys goods properly, fittingly, in an ordered (noble or beautiful) way.

But what of virtues such as courage, moderation, and greatness of soul? As with other virtues, vice is possible. Virtue requires training. Once one sees the measured choice, other choices are ignoble or ugly. But is the virtuous choice implicit even in the error? Part of the experience of pleasure is a filling, and, hence, an over- or underfilling, or an immediate experience of sweetness or beauty and, hence, a proper concentration—one that is neither cloying and excessive nor diffuse and deficient. The unfit experience points to the measured one. The experience of fear, of not being able to stand in place, settle down, know where to turn (and of the fearsome as what is arriving quickly or slowly, expectedly or unexpectedly, from a surprising or unsurprising place), is also an experience of the steadiness that is its counter. The experience of love or friendship is an experience not only of attraction, protection, enjoyment, and common effort but also of fitting (or unfitting) attraction and protection, what should, should not, and need not be done. The experience of receiving honor and praise is at the same time an experience of undeserved or bogus praise: its emptiness is recognized even if it is ignored.

This suggests that human experience is inseparable from reason.[19] All such experience belongs to combining (joining) and separating and, therefore, to a more or less complete joining and separating, relevant to the experience. It is for this reason also that any single experience points to others to which it is attached: courageous actions are connected to a community's requirement of courage in war, for example, and to areas other than war where fear exists and we can overcome it courageously. Even the most immediate short-lived pleasure is experienced as pleasure, and if we are to pursue it we must identify it as this, not that.[20]

This is not to say that we do not choose wrong action or that we cannot encourage right action through law. The complexity and multiplicity of the contexts in which we exercise our powers, the variety of the venues in which we can enjoy them and their related goods and attractions, and the interplay of these factors make error inevitable and legal direction necessary. It is merely to say that not only speech but also our abilities to enjoy goods and limit dangers announce something of their own sufficiency when we experience and employ them, especially as they involve joining, separating, fit, and concentration.

Virtue and Regimes

As I just remarked, the complexity of venues and contexts in which we exercise our powers affects our understanding and experience. There is variety among ways of life and in the implicit view of movement, separating, and combining involved in them: understanding and, therefore, experiencing what is fitting, fulfilling, and independent vary to some extent.

This means that experiencing virtues also varies somewhat among regimes or ways of life. Virtue is connected to the degree of access to the goods and passions it measures and chooses—to the equality of people's claims to them, to the freedom and self-understanding of the "I" who experiences them, and to the way in which goods first approach us as good—guiding us as noble, satisfactory, merely pleasant, or holy.

In classical virtue, goods approach us as available for noble measuring, shaping, or control; that is, they approach us as possibly fulfilling, as available for my noble action. But they also approach in their own power as well as being available for beautiful purposes and satisfactions. These satisfactions and purposes differ from the restlessness of modern desire, the modern generality of pleasure, and the modern wish for security and certainty. This classical approach is true for classical democracy as well as for aristocracy, although it is true in democracy for fewer things—no equal magnificence or greatness of soul is possible—and there is more freedom for the choiceworthiness of physical pleasure. Even in classical democracy as well as aristocratically, however, pleasure is more subtle and satisfactory than is modern democracy's restless relief from unease, because we experience it differently in different activities. We can rank pleasures in relation to pleasing activities; some can be unmixed in the way that seeing something beautiful or acting properly pleases without a preceding lack; and pleasure can involve the experience of burgeoning and fitting properly into place (of fulfilling), as do producing or experiencing what is beautiful, or using office honorably.[21]

We can develop our discussion of the difference between the classical and the modern by considering specific virtues. Aristotle's great pride is related to positions of honor that are open to few, and to a self-understanding of one's merits that would at best be imaginary for most. The related virtue in liberal democracy is responsibility, taking charge to bring about a successful result in a context where each position is in principle open to all, and in which widening one's responsibility is widening one's freedom. A magnificent classical display for a public festival or in war differs from impressive private spending by a modern philanthropist. Intending to obey a universal moral law in the modern way is an equality in righteous behavior that differs from classically unequal prudence. The liberal democratic virtues of industriousness, tolerance, and civility differ in their generality from political and military effort, piety, and aristocratic friendliness or noblesse oblige. The proper, virtuous, experiences of honor, wealth, beauty, and friendship (love) differ, given the difference between our modern conditions of equal competition and access and the presence of slavery and women's political inequality in classical democracies and aristocracies.

Yet how much do or could the virtues truly differ? In one sense, the experience of goods in both classical and modern virtue suggests or points to proper or virtuous experience within their way of life. All tasks in liberalism rest on and point to responsibility, religious belief in liberal democracy rests on and points to public tolerance, and pursuit of wealth in liberal democracy rests on and points to competitive access, even when one acts contrary to these conditions. These indications belong to the equal trust that sets the path of everyday liberal democratic life. Our goods are released as equal possibilities for the relief from unease, within a political community that is formed by justice as equal access. Still, if there is commonality among our human powers, then however much differences in regimes suffuse our experiences, this commonality of powers points to and rests on a possible and ultimately commonly understandable excellence. Each element of our activity—freedom, virtue, benefit, use, and justice—indicates its fullest experience or most complete understanding or, at least, points to commensurable terms for understanding. Possibility (or "power") suffuses actuality, and the highest actuality shows the fullest possibility. The understanding of goodness, justice, and virtue that forms the best classical lives and regimes is the standard by which the other regimes should be measured.[22]

PROPERTY

Property is another central concept, political because of choices about permissible ownership. As with power, it also has a broader meaning: we call what we are composed of our "properties" as well as our powers and abilities. Something's defining elements are its properties.

Property is especially interesting because it is a visible place where we humanize ordinary material (most clearly the land and what grows on it), where we transform it or take it up into what is human, where we limit, rearrange, and even to some degree bring out and develop its elements and give them added meaning. Property is also significant because holding it is a phenomenon that shows an evident link to the political context to which it belongs and to the nature and substance of the goods we seek.

What do we mean by "property"? Let me list some uses. That's my (his) property: I own it. I have property (ownership, land) in that place. That's mine, that's my property, you can't take it from me. Life, liberty, and property. Private property: no trespassing. Stealing, protecting, amassing, earning property. A man of property. Wood's properties.

The leading meaning of property is ownership, what is one's own, what belongs to one, what is mine, what cannot rightfully be separated or detached from me—hence, the significance of protecting one's property. Property is first of all land, "real" property, "real" estate, as opposed, say, to currency, jewelry, or even the buildings one develops on the land, one's "properties." What is "proper" is what is fitting or belonging, and something's properties are what belongs to it, intrinsically. So property is what is one's own, what belongs to something or cannot (rightly) be separated from it without destroying or harming it.

We should also note other dimensions of property. One is the importance of law in determining who owns what; valid claims and contracts are paramount within a country, although less so among countries. So is property primarily or exclusively conventional, or does it have a natural base? This question also comes to light when one recognizes that when something becomes my property (legally or naturally) I change its behavior as it is simply on its own. By nature, the land is what it is and belongs to no one. Yet we, too, are natural, if not only natural. And other animals also take things from their own place as squirrels do acorns from oaks and the soil beneath them, although they may not use them in a human or "creative" manner. Making something my or our property is a central way in which we transform what stands on its own: powers are unlocked that show themselves fully or at all only after human action. Some of what human use brings forward follows the natural generation and shape of the land and what is on it: eating what is there or agricultural cultivation. Much that property allows to be brought forward, however, the use of minerals, metals, and what become energy resources, is novel. The general point is that owning "property" is a human relationship to things, to land primarily, that forms, directs, and unlocks what is "there," something's properties and powers.

PROPERTY AND JUSTICE

Is holding individual property natural, conventional, or historical? Who holds it deservedly? What can make something rightly one's own? In principle, the one who uses natural powers or produced qualities best deservedly makes them his own. This is the substance of justice as unequal to unequals. Such a notion is difficult or even dangerous to implement in practice, however, because it is hard to agree on best use. The best violin should be owned by the best violinist, but who in practice is to judge this? Who in practice is to judge when we speak even more broadly of the best use of land? Who will not claim ownership under such standards? Yet this difficulty does not make the standard less real or make the practical problem simply insoluble, as opposed to perfectly soluble.[23]

Plato offers the solution in principle in the *Republic*—rule of the wise—and also suggests the imperfection of this solution: the wise are not simply wise but, unlike others, know they are ignorant and therefore search for wisdom; that is, they are only partially wise and, consequently, would not wish to spend time distributing property (or other goods and opportunities), which they would do inadequately in any event.[24] More imperfect but also plausible solutions to the practical problem of distributing property according to best use involve rule of the virtuous, that is, rule of those who hold wealth and also have a prudent understanding of the beautiful so that they use their wealth magnificently. Still more imperfect solutions are the actual aristocracies or semi-aristocracies that have existed in fact in Great Britain and Europe. In general, property in these examples is allied with virtue of Aristotle's sort, where what is good is noble and fulfilling, and justice is fitting things together based on inequalities or differences in skill and functions.[25]

This view of justified property—ownership according to best use—is difficult to maintain in practice because of the problems mentioned and the gap between best use and any actual aristocratic rule. It is also limited by insufficiencies of production and by grating inequality or, even, slavery. Nonetheless, the simple clarity of property deservedly belonging to the one who uses it best speaks to the justice of this standard. One would like to recapture it as much as possible in democratic regimes.

The other major justification of property is that one deserves what is one's own simply because it is one's own. Property is rooted in being one's self, being one's own, or in what one needs to be one's own rather than in better or best use. Such property is for us linked to rights, as I discussed earlier, and to the body. The body and its actions are the externalization of oneself as one's own, and the body needs property. This is visible in Locke's understanding of what is common as becoming mine when I mix my labor with it. Otherwise, self-preservation is impossible.[26] Property is the external notice of one's own, one's self, one's preservation, one's rights.

Understanding who might enjoy or use goods most fully may be sufficient to govern distribution for best use (however difficult this distribution is in practice). But it is not sufficient to tell us about the proper recipients of the (equal) goods necessary to be separately spirited, to be one's own. One must also understand the just distribution of goods in conjunction with a dominant view of the individual. For one wants good things for oneself, not only for the one who uses them best. Indeed, some view of the self, of the user and enjoyer, is needed even to justify best use. This understanding of self, moreover, also will involve what other selves deserve: this understanding will to a large degree be connected to differences in regime but not fully.

So holding one's own properly always limits best use simply. Indeed, it is crucial to recognize the split that exists between the good and one's own, as the dangerous religious and "utopian" political attempt to overcome this split show. Above all, the imperfections in any political regime's distribution of goods indicate one element of the excellence of the philosophical life: the link between one's own and the good is most firm when one person's enjoying a good does not detract from another's enjoyment, as is the case with wisdom.

PROPERTY AND LIBERAL DEMOCRACY

There are several implications for justifying property that our own liberal democratic view suggests. Property for us is tied to equality, for the ground of authority is equal will and inviolability, and equal will does not as such point to superior use. In fact, the use of property is largely identical when it means securing and preserving oneself, fleeing death, or reducing unease. The greater force that some may have is not as such a step toward superior use. It is at most a source of short-lived greater competitive success when scarcity exists. Hobbes shows why without enforced law there will always be scarcity and the universal insecurity that results from it: there would be no lasting mastery and none beyond mere preservation; there would at most be a lesser immediate fear of death among some few who are more masterfully spirited. So equal will, when connected to security, becomes the ground of conventionally equal access to property, although the results of this access will be unequal soon enough, as Locke indicates, because of differences in industriousness, rationality, and luck.[27] In the aristocratic world, by contrast, convention is meant to secure and advance inequality based in principle, but never fully in fact, on greater orientation to nobility and honor. These inequalities arise from qualities that are hidden or dormant in a prepolitical "natural" state. The liberal justification of property in terms of an ability to choose and an independence that is largely equal to others, and in terms of being my own as preserving myself, is also connected to the neutral use of property in accumulating goods that relieve unease. Justified property is primarily in terms of what brings about the accumulation of more property.

Property as one's own, and as what deservedly or intrinsically belongs to something, therefore has two central versions among human beings. One is ownership in terms of the capacity for proper use and the correlative unequal spiritedness directed toward honor or distinction. (I am the one who uses these practical goods best and most beautifully.) The other is one's own and ownership in terms of security, preservation, meeting necessity, and relieving unease generally, and the basically equal spiritedness, pride, or will directed to such security. Property may come to differ by degree or fortune, but it requires universal public agreement to secure and establish preservation. In both cases, conventional property, legal property, is meant to secure the conditions for the natural equality or inequality in which it is grounded.

Property and the Body

These points indicate still more about the place of the body in property. One's own is not one's body apart from one's speech or passions, one's soul, the source of movement. But one could hardly do what we do—grasp, feel, produce, and so on—if bodiless. Nor would we have sufficient sensory integrity or separateness, or enjoy or understand the full use of anything's powers.[28] What is crucial in art is beauty, for example, but heard or seen beauty is vital for beauty's full display. The mathematical proportions that are connected to music, and even the unplayed composition in the composer's mind, cannot take the place of what is played and heard. Still, it is the aspiration to beauty that is most crucial in fine art, and although sensual it need not be limited to any particular space: Mozart has had an effect beyond his time and region.

The body is not a mere physical appendage or tool, for "I" feel, see, use, own, and occupy. This is why violations of the body are violations of the person.[29] My property in things and land is suffused with my imprint, although less so in them than in my own body, my lived body. Still, the soul-suffused or lived body is the central reason we require property, either to meet necessity or to use well—to use virtuously—powers and things, some of whose possibilities are brought out only together with the body.

Our bodies, let alone our souls, are less properly interpreted in terms of what is merely physical than one might think. The body is always soul-suffused, even when it deals with its necessities. One sees this in Aristotle's virtues, which are experienced and understood in terms of the right time, that is, not mere neutrally counted time, and in virtues such as just ownership and courage in battle, which are connected to the right space or place, that is, not mere neutrally measured space: virtue does not flee or overstep.

The difference between such human time and space and time and space measured in identical units is a central theme for Heidegger. It is important to see that the human, humanized, or soul-infused body is immersed in and carries before it distances as too near and too far, "space" as the place where something belongs or fits, direction as up above where I hang the painting or down below where I swim, and time as the right time for a discussion, that time when I visited a friend, or now that I am giving a lecture. These must be differentiated from indifferent spatial and temporal units. Such human time and space belong together with (and in that sense are carried along with) my soul, reason, passions, and will.

Something's Properties

Let us further discuss the "properties" of things as a way we point out their characteristics. Something's properties are primarily its speed, weight, how it affects our senses, either when we understand these qualities humanly (a rock is heavy or too heavy to move) or merely materially (a rock weighs five pounds). Such properties ground some of what we can do with things and how they perform the elements of their jobs, so we will sometimes use properties in a manner closely aligned with powers—the properties of this computer as opposed to that one, or the properties of a computer as opposed to a slide rule.

What is a property in its belonging to something? Is it inseparable from it, or does it merely accompany it, as a condition might? Or is it, as with human ownership, sometimes separable but not rightly separated. A property is usually but not necessarily important to something. Nor need it be defining or distinctive.[30] Something's overall form or look or the combination of its properties may be more significant. Nonetheless, a property—and for us, perhaps, rightful property—is intrinsic or is intrinsic in relation to us and not merely an accidental quality or a condition. A thing's properties are intrinsic to it, not (rightly) separable from it, not necessarily, although usually, important for it and not necessarily, although often, distinctive about it. A thing's properties as well as its powers, moreover, become visible and effective in different ways with use, action, or mere observation: when, say, we try to beautify or construct something we uncover various properties of wood or plants. Similarly, human "characteristics" (powers primarily in relation to something's look and form) can also become visible or be allowed to have their presence and effect in different ways.

The experience of things that brings out their powers and properties depends on what allows these activities to occur or to be developed. This is primarily a country's way of life, its law or justice and the understanding of what can be good to which it is directed. This is one reason why political-philosophical matters are so central.

Chapter Four

The Nature of Virtue

Virtue of character is an important purpose or element of political life because it is a vital way we deal with and control goods. It is not the only way, because law is also decisive. Character and law, moreover, are not sufficient to explain how we produce goods, because this often requires art and skill. Which arts and skills we can use to which degree, however, is limited or directed by law and character. So virtue is vital even in production.

Character is connected to an understanding of what makes goods good (their goodness) and to the justice, the proper distribution, that organizes a place's way of life. Pleasures are among these goods: indeed, virtuous behavior is itself said to be pleasant. Character embodies a view of the right way to act and behave. So character, calculations of pleasure, and "oughts" or moral "laws" are linked: the contemporary splits among consequentialist, deontological, and "virtue" ethics are ultimately excessive, however revealing.[1]

The virtues are also a useful place to see that no political community, either concretely or in the regime that forms it, can fully control the experience of its members and citizens. We can address and question virtues through opinions about them, see how true these opinions are, and glimpse how their more complete expression could occur. We observe this procedure in Plato's dialogues. Our experience of virtue also embodies what is questionable in our understanding of it. As I said, our powers indicate something about their proper use even if we ignore these indications.

This, then, sets the direction of my discussion here. I will, first, discuss virtue in relation to goods, second, discuss it in relation to various regimes, third, discuss virtue in relation to morality generally, and, fourth, discuss how the experience and substance of virtue shows both its attraction and its limits. In doing this I will draw on my earlier discussions.

The basic experience of virtue stems from people and things regularly doing their jobs well or poorly, or of their stepping along the right path, doing the proper or "done" thing. In all these cases, we notice some experience of better and worse, good and bad, proper or improper, right or wrong, pure or impure. We may not make these precise distinctions; indeed, as we begin to make them we may see differences between, say, what is right or just and what is best. It is sufficient that we experience better and worse, or the right way (our way) and wrong ways, for virtue to have a ground. It is as "virtue," via fatherly education and concern, that the phenomenon of proper or improper or better and worse among human beings first opens to the classics' philosophical reflection.[2]

Aristotle's Virtues

That different virtues are connected to different goods is the heart of Aristotle's discussion in his *Ethics*.[3] I will begin by following this procedure, although my purpose is not to explicate Aristotle's view. Aristotle's discussion, moreover, seems not to include certain contemporary virtues. So, although I will start from some version of his discussion, I will keep these limits in mind.

Virtues as a group constitute character, and character concerns the way one deals with goods and passions. "Deals with" means enjoys, directs, and uses. The reason Aristotle can say that ethical virtue or good character in action constitutes happiness is because it enjoys and otherwise deals with what is good. Virtue is not an eschewing or rejecting of goods such as pleasure but a way to treat them properly. Moreover, virtues, which command actions and are implicated in them and in thinking, also use our powers. Happiness consists of the most complete or beautiful use of our powers to enjoy the basic goods. This is why virtue is choiceworthy.[4]

Aristotle understands virtue to deal with fears, bodily pleasures, great and lesser wealth, great and lesser honor, anger, the ridiculous, friendliness, speech, law and distribution, love and friendship, and the objects of the intellect. So our virtues are courage, moderation, generosity (or liberality), magnificence, greatness of soul, ambition, proper anger, wit, friendliness, honesty, justice, friendship, and intellectual virtue (understanding). Piety, faith, hope, service, charity, philanthropy, humility, humanity, decency, industriousness, carefulness, tolerance, civility (niceness), and responsibility are not on his lists. Some elements of these virtues could perhaps be included among his, decency in friendliness and justice, say, or humanity in greatness of soul, and charity and philanthropy in generosity and magnificence. But the others are Christian or liberal democratic. Humility is for Aristotle a vice, moreover, and piety is at best subsumed in justice or in spending magnificently to honor the gods. So, although Aristotle's discussion of virtue retains startling power, it is not, for us, obviously complete.

The Experience of Virtue

What does it mean to say that the virtues are connected to experiencing goods? It means more than, indeed it hardly means at all, that the virtues are ways to acquire these goods or are otherwise external to them. If a virtuous disposition enjoys its associated good at the right time and place, with the right people, and in the right amount, then these features belong to the experience of the good. Passions move and goods complete or satisfy. Goods call forth and beckon. Dealt with properly, they satisfy properly. True virtue, as opposed to incomplete virtue or vice, therefore depends on the truth and breadth of our experience and understanding of human powers, and their orientation to what exercises and engages them fully. Narrow or incomplete activity is truncated, unbalanced, and excessive. It is not true that shortcomings in virtue deliver no internal punishment other than the physical discomfort of the immoderate man.[5]

If this is so, why is virtue not the same everywhere, why is it often ignored, and why does attaining it require training and punishment? And what is the path from virtue's associated vices or imperfections to its perfections?

Virtue, good character, requires training and punishment because of human capacities and freedom. The point of human excellence is not only to act correctly, but to choose to act correctly, and to judge what correct action is. Otherwise, human action is not free. Free, reasonable action, however, allows the possibility of error.[6]

But this does not tell us sufficiently why we need training. We need it because acquiring virtue and using the mind well take time and are not automatic. They must be achieved and practiced. One way we achieve them is through persuasion. But persuasion does not explain why we also need punishment, the degree of distance between virtue and vice, or what is sometimes untrue in persuasion. These arise from the variety of regimes and ways of life and, therefore, the unnaturalness of certain "virtues" or modes of proper behavior; from the scarcity of many of the natural goods and, therefore, the need to limit competition and excess; from the insufficiencies of our abilities; from the complexity of many goods; and from the extent of our pride.

Let us consider what appears to be the unnaturalness of certain virtues in the sense that they often go against the grain (and not only when one is young) and that they are not practiced spontaneously. If something is good, why should it have any natural limit? What, for example, could be harmful about seeking too much significant knowledge? The nature of certain goods, however, requires particular attachments—being true in the sense of loyalty and limit. Friendship is an example. The nature of other goods is that they are inherently scarce; political rule is an example. One of the things attractive in them is that not all can have them; they therefore issue in rivalry and require great effort to achieve. So it is highly unlikely that one will possess all such goods. The nature of still other goods is that they require for their pursuit and enjoyment an insufficient use of our powers, say, wealth or physical pleasure. The nature of still others is that the good itself—pleasure in its full variety, beauty, honor, and knowledge—is very complex.

The result of these limits and complexities is that the immediate attractiveness of goods is not simply coherent: some are attractive because they are easy to enjoy with little ability or training, some are attractive because of scarcity that often requires inordinate effort, and some, such as magnificence, deal with goods, such as beauty, that are complex and debatable. There is a disputability in the good or attractive life such that the measured nature of virtue is difficult to achieve. Nonetheless, virtue is real, although complex, because there are (rough) overall measures connected to one's own abilities and attachments, the use or importance of the goods with which one deals in relation to these abilities, and goods' scarcity and complexity. Punishment, persuasion, and direction can and do measure mistakenly but are nonetheless necessary to set one on a right but unfortunately often a wrong path.

The nature of all virtues, some more clearly than others, is that they require a political community. This also limits individual choice and, therefore, requires training. One example, across many regimes, is courage. Courage has a natural, spirited, basis, but as a virtue we must choose it. It deals with a range of fears, but as Aristotle sees it the central fear is of death in battle. This shows the degree to which it is political. That is, it is not sufficiently attractive individually that it can be achieved successfully without training and public support. But this is not to say that it is in no way naturally attractive individually. On the contrary. To someone with strong spiritedness, protecting and taking risks are naturally attractive.

To remember that courage is dealing properly with fear of death in battle is to see how much it is a political virtue, necessary to protect the common good.[7] The other virtues are also significantly common, for either the good with which they deal is largely political, such as honor, or the good that they measure properly flourishes only with common effort and security—wealth and beauty, for example. When goods and virtues are common, however, they become especially subject to persuasion and to force wielded by the most persuasive and strongest. The virtues can then become habits whose exercise keeps one on a path of righteousness that is controlled by others, so that what is not naturally attractive becomes a virtue (asceticism is an example), natural goods are reinterpreted so that my generosity and justice become (mandated) service, and political regimes of only limited justice dominate. The communal nature of virtue is an occasion not only of truth, but of fraud and lies. The possibility of truth is the possibility of error.

Despite this, the justice or lack in one's community and the truth or not of one's "virtues" peek through, or more, in the very experience of them. This is especially obvious when persuasion and discussion and not mere punishment belong to training, because the possibility exists of questioning opinions. This then enables one to see that the fullest versions of the virtue and proper enjoyment of its goods might flourish elsewhere than in one's own way. It also occurs when a community's justice or way of life is brought to sight explicitly, as it is when we consider establishing laws, fight wars, or found communities.[8] The proper balance of goods and various options and limits must then be considered explicitly.

This recognition, however, is primarily discursive. I am claiming that in addition to this, the very experience of one's (insufficiently) "virtuous" enjoyment of goods carries with it its problematic nature in the sense that what one experiences shows its limits in its very attractiveness. Things governed inadequately by virtue appear either cloying or unsatisfactory and not sufficiently alluring or independent. In this way they point to what is more adequate, much as discussion and questioning does.

Another way to see this is by considering the fact that enjoying goods is, as I have said, always to a degree "noetic" or intellectual. It involves seeing something general as and before one pursues or enjoys it in particular. So, for example, one sees what a generous act is before, or as, one is performing a particular act of generosity or recognizes that an advance or retreat is courageous in order to choose it freely and stay with it. Enjoying goods involves dividing and combining, so that to enjoy, say, what is beautiful is both to see what is not beautiful and to see how beautiful things are fittingly organized and placed. Enjoying goods involves seeing what largely stands on its own and what does not, so that we grasp the noble, beautiful, or high. It involves recognizing that more, or more of the same, remains to be enjoyed, so that one senses the adequate and inadequate. It involves seeing what is closer to a perfect or satisfactory version of what one is enjoying, as one recognizes that something is a more lasting and less fleeting, a more general and less idiosyncratic, and a more complete and less truncated instance of beauty, honor, generosity, or pleasure. Indeed, this "seeing" is not only seeing before and after, or even seeing along with. It is also the seeing, that is, the discriminating, the articulating, the revealing, involved in feeling and in directing feeling. It is the heart of long-lasting satisfaction in activities, including bodily activities, which are for us not merely physical, but, as we have said, humanized, rationalized, "soul-suffused." What shows itself in an action to be most complete, subtly and complexly organized, and compellingly independent is the more virtuous version of it, and the virtues that deal with the more complex goods are the higher among the virtues: the statesman's greatness of soul and prudence are superior to the moderation in pleasure of the temperate man and show themselves even in ordinary political actions as their model, inspiration, and goal. This showing can be faint or easy to ignore, but it will be present, because each of our experiences is noetic. The partial experience of virtue and, indeed, of vice points to true or complete virtue.

Virtue and Liberal Democracy

I have suggested that the virtues are connected to political regimes, or ways of life. This becomes especially clear when we consider the variety of virtues that appear after Aristotle's discussion. To experience humility as excessive modesty about the honors one deserves, to experience it as a defect of pride, differs from experiencing it as a virtue of proper subservience. The experience is embedded in a general world or atmosphere of divine authority and the proper steps to lead a pious life. Responsibility and industriousness are virtues connected to securing equal rights and achieving success in a regime of equal opportunities. So one does not see them in this way in Aristotle.

Virtues are connected to different regimes for three central reasons: the understanding of justice that constitutes the regime, the basic experience of good that is involved with the regime and its virtues, and the nature of the "I" and freedom coordinate with the regime. Complex as this may seem, however, one can still open in any regime to the other or truer experience.

I have mentioned virtues other than Aristotle's, notably the Christian virtues and the liberal democratic or "bourgeois" virtues, and I will now discuss our modern virtues more fully. The most significant liberal virtues are industriousness, tolerance, responsibility, and civility, or, in its softer or more debased form, niceness. They are virtues because we habitually choose actions in accord with them. Actions in accord with them are not calculations, such as self-interest rightly understood or the judgment that crime doesn't pay. Rather, they are habits or dispositions that are followed by judgment and choice. They belong to the trust, to the implicit expectations, in liberal regimes: we expect that others will develop the habits that allow them to succeed, work hard, and be tolerant, publicly, of religions of which they disapprove.

These liberal virtues are necessary to succeed in a regime where the one who enjoys goods is the individual holder of rights, equal to others and deserving no special privileges. Responsibility, especially, is the virtue that allows one to rely on oneself. It is advanced by discipline and by the reasonable accumulation of resources—attending to one's interests. Responsibility is the virtue that tries to brings matters to a successful conclusion and, therefore, often helps others as well as oneself. A responsible man or woman is accountable for success: he holds himself accountable, so others may also hold him accountable. It is precisely responsible people whom we wish to hire privately and to whom we look to accomplish public tasks. Responsibility alone is insufficient for success: one also needs skills. But it is part of responsibility to acquire the appropriate skills and to husband the resources that allow further resources to be accumulated.

Responsibility is a necessary virtue when, as in liberal democracy, almost all tasks are in principle and often in fact open to anyone, and what is good publicly presents itself not as something rare but as what can satisfy desire or relieve unease. It is an egalitarian analogue to great pride. But responsibility is not a virtue that we each experience in equal measure, because although one can attempt to make oneself responsible for the successful outcome of greater and greater tasks, most will not do so. In the usual situations, responsibility is more restricted than it is in great economic and political efforts. To exercise greater responsibility may seem to hem one in, but in fact it increases freedom by expanding mastery—by placing one thoughtfully within a wider and wider field. The absence of responsibilities is not self-direction but nondirection.

Industriousness is also a liberal democratic virtue grounded in equal rights and the public equality of pleasures. One can be industrious about anything. Equal hard work to accumulate wealth for (possible) pleasant use is not a classical virtue. The ancients did not favor laziness, of course, but they did favor intelligently used leisure and a political and courageous life rather than the useful arts. They experienced the goodness of things together with their beauty: virtue is noble. Similarly, civility differs from aristocratic friendliness because it suggests an equal right to be heard or to receive equally distributed opportunities, sometimes with little regard for merit. (Everyone deserves a chance to speak, which is reasonable in a democracy and counters the usual inflated claims to special treatment.) Tolerance is the virtue that concerns the public treatment of those with other beliefs once religious beliefs are considered to be private choices and, thus, equal from the public point of view. Tolerance differs from piety, the traditional religious virtue, a disposition to observe a particular set of public commands and observances in relation to the gods and what is holy that brooks no rivals and belongs to public law.[9]

These liberal virtues do not preclude the classical virtues, but the equality of rights and opportunities they serve and from which they stem affects the public presence and importance of these virtues. It especially alters the least egalitarian among them. In liberal democracy, what might have been greatness of soul is seen, and the one who has it largely sees himself, as being politically responsible yet basically equal, and magnificence becomes at one end the duty of philanthropy and at the other attention to music and art that is governed by a principle of equality of access and taste.

The dominance in liberal democracies and other regimes of a single public understanding of the goodness of goods, justice, and freedom does not eliminate, although it deeply affects, the possibility of other understandings. As I am suggesting, any presence of the good, just, and noble shows its incompleteness but also carries the elements of its own (degree of) choiceworthiness, bindingness, and coherence within its way of life.[10]

Virtue, Morality, and Justice

When people today discuss ethics from the perspective of virtue they often think of morality. Practical or ethical virtues as distinguished from intellectual ones are "moral" virtues. The standpoint of what one ought to do is "morality." The virtues, or some virtues such as justice and responsibility, are thought to be duties.

"Moral" behavior seems to be less about properly enjoying goods and passions than about restricting one's actions in order to benefit others but not necessarily oneself. It is "immoral" to lie or steal even if the lie advances one or the stolen goods would be enjoyable. And the moral action is not as such intrinsically pleasant. But the classically virtuous act is intrinsically pleasant or beautiful and, more, its proper or measured enjoyment is just that, enjoyment, rather than a check on enjoyment.

Morality in this sense is close to law as a command followed by punishment for disobeying the command. In this way it is allied with part of justice — only part because justice generally is a disposition to act justly, which involves the practical wisdom to choose just actions and laws and not only to obey law. Just laws and actions are those that link and distribute (or permit the distribution of) goods and tasks in accord with the implicit (or explicit) understanding of what constitutes a common good. Justice is the disposition to discover, command, and follow (obey) the proper distribution of goods and opportunities to those to whom they should belong, namely, those who will use them best or those who must own them, given an understanding of freedom and what is good.[11]

Not all purportedly just action takes the form of law, of legal command and obeying commands. But much does, especially when public punishment seems necessary to ensure obedience. Morality, when seen as a series of injunctions not to lie, steal, and so on, that brook no exceptions and require little judgment to apply fits together with justice as legality. Legality that covers all citizens equally or, indeed, all human or rational beings equally is coherent with freedom as equal rights. Indeed, when one considers religious actions commanded by law—the old and new laws or sharia law—one sees still another aspect to morality. The laws command steps, actions, ways, staying on the proper path, not with an orientation to enjoyment, but as its own goal: justice as righteousness (the pious self) attained by following the correct path.[12]

MORALITY AND LIBERAL DEMOCRACY

Moral laws and religious ways are, thus, related, for acting morally as obeying moral law means stepping along the correct path, acting correctly without attending primarily to outcomes, and doing so equally. Indeed, modern moral law proves to be especially coordinated with the world of actual and incipient liberal democracy. By this I mean that Kant's view of the moral law is grounded on the freedom of equal individuals as those who have rightful individual authority, those who deserve equal respect. Moral action is as such divorced from the actual attainment or enjoyment of goods and pleasures, but modern morality and pleasure are nonetheless linked.

The liberal view of pleasure with which the modern moral law is coordinated is pleasure as relief from unease. It is a view in which all pleasures are equal, so what is best is more. One difficulty with this notion is its narrow view of happiness and of pleasure itself. In the classical and (partially) commonsense view, pleasures are connected to activities and virtues in ways that do not allow pleasures to be simply stripped from them and summed up independently as pleasure. In the classical view, moreover, pleasure also involves fulfillment, burgeoning, and immediate delight (e.g., of seeing someone or something beautiful) and not only indifferently filling what is empty, or relieving unease.[13]

A second difficulty with the liberal view of pleasure is ambiguity about the subject who experiences happiness. For if the common good is simply what conduces to the greatest pleasure of the citizenry as a whole we can presumably ignore any particular individual or even large numbers of them as long as some total amount of pleasure is greater in the community.

The security against this possible tyranny of the citizenry or majority is to protect individual rights. But we justify rights on the basis of each person's unavoidable self-direction, grounded on ordinary will, free deliberation, choice, and action. It is possible or plausible to attempt to sweep this very independence into the calculus of pleasure and simply to use or ignore various individuals. What matters is the totality of preferences, including the preference for being and remaining free. Rights might then seem not to be defined by any special inviolability but merely to be an element of pleasure as its resting point and, therefore, absorbed into calculations about it. "Morality," or the moral law, in contrast, is a free act of what appears to transcend or leap ahead of any natural will, and this free act belongs to us all equally. The calculus of pleasure (or any good) must, in this (Kantian) view, find its place within the moral law, which is said to stem from or be coordinated with the dignity or self-respect in each of us. In these ways, a basic unity can be maintained among individual rights, happiness as satisfaction of desire, and the moral law without sacrificing the individual.[14]

The first problem with this powerful view is its arbitrariness or incompleteness and, hence, its implausibility. Kant's moral law concerns practical reason as allowing certain facts or actions (lying or not lying, for example) to be willed or formed morally. In his view, this requires that moral reason and will be pure, independent of what is "natural," empirical, pleasurable. No sensible intuition is required or can be permitted if there is to be a moral law that can determine our will. By contrast, purely intuited space and time allow us to organize sense impressions and, together with projected (transcendental) understanding, allow us to grasp (or impose) causal and other ordering relations among things. Still, causal order does not exist within things or impressions, or have natural meaning apart from them, although we cannot experience them without imposing this order.

But what does the pure moral law organize or moralize? From where do its moral commands obtain their meaning? For Kant, it is our elementary moral views and acts, our believing it to be wrong, say, to lie and steal. But these views and acts are not analogous to basic impressions (as we can try to break things down to them even if, pace Kant, they are not what we sensibly experience initially). Rather, "moral" acts are already meaningful and disputable: the views and acts whose possibility Kant tries to establish through his moral laws, the views and acts his moral law interprets and explains, are not universal or even elementary. He begins with a certain experience or group of experiences and remains with this beginning.

The second problem is Kant's constricted view of freedom. To strictly separate us from being materially caused and, therefore, to step away from a summative calculus in which I can justify using you (or myself) because it adds to some total good, one might show that individuals are free in the sense that we are not determined by a natural causal chain. Kant attempts to do this. But such freedom need not be (only) the universal legislating that Kant has in mind in which we are our own efficient cause. Rather, freedom as not being naturally determined could well involve any use of reason to form, separate, and combine, or any nonperceptible act involving nonperceptible things. Practical reason or freedom can see, acknowledge, arrange, and rearrange ends and satisfactions as freely as it can (attempt to) act as if choosing a means to its end could be universally legislated. In any event, Kant does not clarify why this cannot be.

Another peculiarity here is that the coordination of Kantian morality and the grounds of liberal democracy is largely seen in terms of pleasure in the narrow utilitarian sense, without a clear discussion of why this should be so.[15]

The upshot of these points concerning Kant's morality (even if my criticisms are incorrect) is that the moral law replaces rights as the effective meaning of individual separateness and inviolability: rights remain equal politically but are based on this revised view and apply only in particular areas. The effect as well is to make justice (ordinary law) stricter in its presumed political equality so that following and administering law begins to separate itself from its purpose—advancing the common good—and increasingly becomes a matter of strict proceduralism.[16] Political law, the moral law, and pleasure are indeed coordinated here and fit coherently. But this order gives short shrift to the place of character in government, downplays virtue as the proper way to experience goods (and not merely, as morality does, to control our access to them), and has a too strict and ultimately unconvincing view of what ought to be, of inviolability (respect), and of legality.

What is "moral," thus, is based on an arbitrary or insufficient understanding of freedom and does not in fact tell us what ought to be where what is good is not simply what is pleasant or where each of us is not ethically equal. Rather, for this, a certain kind of character, which, of course, may publicly and privately choose actions close to moral absolutes, is vital.

The so-called moral law suffers theoretically from the questions I raised. We also experience these issues practically. For if we treat the moral law as a set of unbreakable demands, its excesses, its imprudence, become pressing. It sometimes seems wrong not to lie or steal—when the harms to others are great. The split between the "right" way to act and predictably harmful results is too vast actually to be ethically proper. Morality in this sense reveals its extremism, its link to religious ways, and, especially, its link to the wish for certainty. It is especially when one might in fact be treating others as inviolable that moral universality, perhaps paradoxically, falls short—the lie needed to save someone from the secret police or the stealing necessary to save the starving. Similarly, the judgment we require for excellence, and which belongs to the full use of the mind, is underdeveloped in a world of moral universal absolutes. On the whole, liberal democracy, its ground in natural rights, its characteristic virtues, and its predating the absolute moral law of Kant and his successors, is a superior and less fantastic combination of proper choice, satisfaction, and each individual's inviolability.

THE RANGE OF THE VIRTUES

The major question to which the virtues point is the degree and status of their truth. Let us say that courage is proper action with regard to fear in war: not giving in, breaking ranks, being immobile, or risking a thoughtless forward charge. Rather, one risks or gives in in the right way, time, and place, with the right companions. Let us say that to be moderate is to satisfy physical desire in the right way, time, and place, with the right people; to be magnificent is to spend beautifully in the right way; and greatness of soul is to seek and enjoy positions of honor properly. There is a link among these Aristotelian virtues and aristocracies much as there is a link among liberal democratic virtues such as responsibility and justice grounded in equal rights, what is good seen as pleasure that relieves unease, and the common good understood as securing equal rights and expanding the material available for satisfaction.

The link in the case of courage, moderation, magnificence, greatness of soul, and Aristotle's other virtues is to justice grounded in unequal prudence and political freedom, what is good seen as completeness or sufficiency (what is noble) and as using our abilities actively to experience such sufficiency, and the common good understood as connecting and limiting ends. This link, however, cannot disguise the questionability of the virtues, in their own terms.[17] For what is the measured amount? What are the beautiful things or true honors, or the true fears and satisfactions? What is their proper venue? These questions spur the perplexities about the virtues that we see in Plato's dialogues, which raise questions about the truth of the goods with which the virtues deal—what truly is beauty, pleasure, or wealth?—and about the virtues—what truly is love or friendship, justice or wisdom? Plato's discussions, moreover, are more visibly extreme than Aristotle's. They raise questions about possible conflicts among virtues (does knowledge so reduce fear that courage disappears?), the seeming inferiority of political science, with its uncertain subject matter, to any concrete art, and the proper location of justice: is it in the soul or the city?[18]

These discussions bring out the important fact that what is virtuous and what the virtuous objects are become more visible once we consider the insufficiency, imprecision, and unclarity of any opinion we have about a virtue, or our experience of it. Courage cannot mean never retreating if this leads to defeat or if one recklessly disobeys an order meant to husband forces for a more significant battle. It does not mean standing firm in every situation. Nor can it always involve risk if patient action allows taking future risks that are more likely to succeed in important encounters. Moderation may mean limiting some appropriate physical pleasures to attend to greater beauty. Although the beautiful may be pleasant, however, not everything pleasant is fitting, and not everything pleasant and fitting belongs together with what is striking and outstanding.[19] Courageous, moderate, and generous actions may be restricted by the way a community produces and distributes resources and the kind of equality it considers to be just. And what seems financially generous loses its virtuous luster if the gift is misused. All these issues lead to the dizzying inadequacies that Socrates is always able to expose in any opinion about the virtues. Ultimately, what any virtue is, or its "idea," involves separating and combining, protecting and enjoying, in the many areas in which the good or passion with which the virtue is involved exists: from financial generosity or sensual moderation through courageous defense of the city and the prudent arranging of the city's goods to love and friendship.

In each case, the inability of a virtue to be fully clarified and stabilized intellectually in relation to its ordinary sphere of private and political action leads to a presentation at a more complete level. The ordinary levels are images of the fuller level in the sense that the virtue can show its full power and deal with its objects in their full powers only at the fuller, more complex, levels, much as a shadow looks like but cannot otherwise act as what casts it.

These tensions are still further complicated by the fact that, say, courage of the intellect cannot simply encompass risk in war, intellectual liberality encompass financial generosity, or love of scientific or universal knowledge encompass love of one here and now. The virtues intellectually are more complete than they are ethically and politically, more subtle and complex in their reasoning and in separating and combining things and possibilities. But they are not identical to the usual virtue in its usual field. Moreover, ordering and arranging goods politically varies by regime, so that, say, the initial or usual moderation or generosity may be much more abstemious in one than another or the initial courage more vigorous. Implicit trust, expectation, and individual independence vary, as does the degree to which goods — pleasure, say — and their virtues are allowed to be liberated or to become respectable. Moreover, the rank or importance of a virtue may vary or be transformed in different regimes, as great pride is lowered by us to responsibility when it is not condemned simply, magnificence to responsible philanthropy or service, piety to tolerance, or moderation to accumulation and investment. Indeed, these complexities are extended by the fact that the understanding or liberating of the "self" who is virtuous will vary, as will the initial experience of what is good, the goodness that governs the approach as good of good things.

The result is complexity in measuring and understanding. Nevertheless, we can reduce this complexity because, as I have argued, we can compare the justice of different ways of life — the wholeness or completion within which virtues and other elements are experienced and active — in terms of their sufficiency and precision; the goods, activities, and human powers they leave out, narrow, or overemphasize; and these goods' and activities' proper fit, order, or importance. One can also engage in this comparison by considering the goods with which the virtues deal, their measured separating and combining, even somewhat apart from the regimes. A virtue's meaning, the intelligibility and the guidance it offers, is not fully regime dependent, as I indicated with liberal democracy. This is also true of who "I" am. The common heart of each of the virtues is how they shape and elevate our experience of goods and passions and allow them to flourish separately and together with each other, and how they allow "me" to flourish.

VIRTUE AND THE INDIVIDUAL

We should, thus, reflect more fully here on individual as distinguished from common experience. If I am asked to be courageous,

"I" am asked to be courageous. As I said earlier, what "I" am is primarily my soul, not my body, or my body suffused with my soul, where the description of my body—bulk, extension, shape, existence in time—must chiefly be in meaningful, not neutral, terms, even to a large degree when I am meeting my bodily necessities. To say the body is suffused with soul is to say primarily that it is suffused with reason, not directed by separate sense perceptions, but by the things or matters that we know or opine and (commonly) sense.

It is also to say that the body is suffused with the passions as movements of reaching out and bringing back, together with reason. "I" am primarily the experience of spiritedness, self-containment, and pride, and of (self-)love, elevation, and reverence for my possible excellence and completeness. As I argued earlier, a notion of "I" or "identity," as an interpretation of spiritedness and self-elevation, fits within a regime's context of trust and expectations. It also opens to various areas within any way of life where the good or passion that a virtue controls can appear: this allows me to see how to expand from a less to a more complete and just experience of a virtue. My identity involves my lived body, property, and the presentation to me of my alternatives and possible excellence. Indeed, these alternatives are available to attract me not only within my own way of life but also in more general or cosmopolitan terms, with differing degrees of clarity.[20] As "particular," as experiencing (my) movement and intellectual combining and discriminating, I necessarily, if implicitly, project and am immersed in something whole, which is what ultimately permits more specific intelligibility and guidance.[21] Loyalty to myself and to my particular community is at the same time immersion, if unnoticed, in what is general, comprehensive, and excellent: what is good simply as well as one's own.[22]

Coeval with movement, one experiences oneself—is oneself—as lack: I am ignorant, for example, and wish to know. And one also experiences oneself as enclosed and possibly threatened and thus as stiffening, repelling, and incorporating, as prideful. One's "out to" is toward what beckons (attracts), in order to combine with or ascend to it. This "out to" is out from what discovers itself to be needy (by seeing a beauty greater than itself, say) to what satisfies. But one cannot fully merge with the beautiful, the good, and the whole of things. One is always incomplete, and there are greater beckoning wholes. Nor can one fully master or possess what is independent. One cannot even be fully responsible where there are equals, as in liberal democracies. So the experience of myself and my powers is also always one of incompletion—continued eros and pride that does not fully master what it tries to incorporate. But how aware one is of this varies.[23]

In this sense, the fullest, although still incomplete, "I" would be the cosmopolitan I, the philosophical I, and the fullest virtue would be philosophical virtue. Yet each "I," and not only the cosmopolitan one, is in some way inviolable—deserving of treatment as free, responsible, and educable. "I" am movement, lack (openness, question), and enclosure, a movement out and bringing back (as much as is possible) by (and for) our full capacities to their correlate (what is, and is good.)

This is not to suggest, however, that any virtue can somehow ignore or simply vault beyond the political community. Most goods require politics to be produced, understood, or enjoyed. Indeed, a particular community is sometimes more visibly open to what is general than are its individual members, because unlike an individual a community does not always or directly experience (its own) movement, and its "body" is sometimes only the changeable place of its happening. Its forms can sometimes be seen to be not only its own, and, therefore, many of my possibilities within a community may come to light more generally (e.g., as "virtue") than they would for me individually. What this suggests, again, is that the virtues are initially and for the most part connected to political regimes, or ways of life. Responsibility and industriousness are virtues connected to securing equal rights and achieving success in a regime of equal opportunities. Greatness of soul, great pride, is the most complete practical virtue in a regime that is dedicated to what is noble. To experience humility as excessive modesty about the honors one deserves, to experience it as a defect of pride, differs from experiencing it as a virtue of proper subservience. The experience of humility as proper service is embedded in a universal world or atmosphere of divine authority and the proper steps to take to lead a pious life.

Chapter Five

The Nature of
What Is Common

I have said that the contexts from which actions and things draw their ordinary and initial meaning involve two matters primarily. One is the first presentation of what allows us to deal with things as good, worthwhile, worth pursuing, choiceworthy. This is their "goodness," and is clearly connected but not identical to judging the actually good things. The second is the equal and unequal distribution of tasks, opportunities, and goods and their fit or working together, what is proper to be done, by whom. This fit is not simply automatic but also requires virtue and law. Assuring this distributive and legal justice is the chief task of political and legislative science. Together, the fit of tasks and opportunities to achieve certain goods constitutes what we hold in common in a way of life. This meaning grounds the basic trust and expectations among citizens that is the heart of how we conduct ourselves and what we take for granted every day.

We first experience most matters together with others—learning about words and things, common endeavors and enjoyments, staying along the proper or righteous path as one learns it from elders. How "I" distinguish myself and am allowed to develop my distinctiveness also differs in many but not all ways in different ways of life.[1] The understanding and balance among one's own (is one the noble or possibly excellent soul, the holder of rights, the distinctive self, the pious supplicant?), what is good, our own (this people), and justice differ in different regimes.

Varieties of Commonality

Explicit conceptual concern about the common qua common depends on these first experiences and how we bring them to light—the way we separate and combine, especially, of course, in language. Explicit discussion is linked to an implicit grasp of the varieties of commonality. Understood properly, indeed, abstract forms as reason sees them are what make particular experiences possible.

We make things common (or join them) or notice their commonality in several ways. One can agglomerate things or cover them (or see that they are agglomerated or covered), say, by randomly piling rocks, or rocks and leaves, or by covering each item under a tent, whether the items are otherwise similar or different. One can see that things are permeated with the same quality, as daylight permeates all during the day. In this case, the members may differ in degree, for example, in brightness, or be agglomerated randomly.

One can join things not only by piling, covering, and permeating (or internally reflecting) but also by linking, stitching, gluing, fastening, tying, and weaving them, as one would link the links in a chain or in a historical process, stitch the pieces of a garment, nail together two boards or see that they are linked, glued, or layered. This joining can be ordered linking in which each member must be in its place, as with links in a process or sewn garment, or it can be disordered agglomerating, as when one nails together two boards randomly.[2] One can also join by unifying things or seeing that they are unified, as one sees the unity in different instances of something—say, that each chair is or is called "chair." Here, the unity involves the same things (because only chairs can be ordered as chairs), but it is not obviously one in which the parts—the many chairs—fit together or are ordered or arranged.

One can also join by forming, organizing, arranging, distributing, or placing things or seeing that they are arranged, as different members are organized into a team, different parts of a face belong to it, new coins fill a collection's gap, or one piece of cake is shared among several people. One can join as well by modeling or measuring things or seeing that they are images, as copies of a picture or model imitate it, your shadow is modeled on you, or family members resemble each other through the cast of their face or by each having one or two of the same prominent features.[3] The model or standard does not merely agglomerate its images; there is an ordered connection.[4]

One can also join by incorporating or possessing. When we incorporate or possess things or see that they are incorporated they lose their independence as do, say, food in a body or conquered land. In these examples, we make things our own: owning or possessing is another form of joining. It is unifying as separating—say, as protecting or defending, or bringing back. In terms of the elements as unified we may speak of holding and what is held, surrounding or protecting and what is protected, securing and what is secured, and owning and what is owned. In similar ways, those that belong to a whole are parts as members, instances, examples, images, particulars, and pieces.

Correlated to ways things are common or belong together are ways they are absent or missing. This is especially relevant when parts are absent from wholes, such as a missing link in a chain, a missing player in a game, or a missing loved one.[5]

COMMON ORGANIZATIONS

When one thinks of political communities one thinks first of their likeness to common organizations or arrangements: teams and orchestras, for example, or faces and their parts.[6] If we examine this further we see that the parts of an organized common, a whole, can differ or be the same in their power and activity (violins differ from cellos, and each violin or cello differs from the others); can differ in different ways (the strings differ from the woodwinds); can be equally or unequally significant (the conductor is more important than the violist at the last desk); and can be equally or unequally replaceable or interchangeable (the concert master is more difficult to replace than one of the second violinists).[7] Wholes can be separate and independent (a chair, a team, an orchestra) or semi-independent (the chair in the room, the orchestra among other orchestras, my face together with my body). The whole and its parts may itself be a model or an image—the exemplary orchestra and the mediocre one.

The parts of an organized common, moreover, can participate in it or be connected with it in different ways. The central type of participation is to fit, even if imperfectly, as do the members of the team, orchestra, or parts of a face. The parts are arranged or arrange themselves within the whole so that it reaches its goal, does its job well, or appears beautiful or appropriate.

Another element of common units such as teams and orchestras is that through them we produce something in common. That is, we make or bring forward products that could not come from one of us alone—an orchestra's music and harmonies, for example. In some cases, the common product—say, a beautiful sound—is intrinsic to the activity, not an after the fact good. In other cases it is separate—the automobile produced in the factory and sent on its way rather than the action of producing it, or the team's victory as opposed merely to the pleasure of playing the game. Usually, the common effort needs direction, although it may sometimes be (or seem) spontaneous.

What is common through organizing and arranging will normally need all its parts, but some instances of what is common may not. A good orchestra needs all sections to be at their best, although it may not need every one of its particular players. But the "2" that is universal to its identical instances (that covers them all equally) does not need any one of the 2s. One might then wonder whether a model needs its images—not to be itself fully, but to show the full range of its powers in partial situations, as one might learn that and how I can cast my shadow without my being less myself if I never find myself in a situation where my shadow is cast.[8]

We should also see that in an organized whole the whole will (usually) differ in power or activity from the part, whether or not its parts are identical. Consider, for example, the same piece of wood shaped differently into a table or a chair; or a repertory company, where the same actors (the parts) differ in different plays and the performance differs from the actors; or a soul, which, as a whole, differs from any of its powers; or the excellence of a team, which differs from the skills of its members.

All these differences are relevant for different political communities, which are limited or formed by these more abstract possibilities. For the modes of commonality are connected to justice as distribution, order, and ownership. Trust and communication invigorate commonality and bring together organized parts.

POLITICAL COMMONS AND CITIZENSHIP

As I suggested, we first experience most matters together with others—common endeavors, the proper or righteous path, common life. Even how "I" distinguish myself differs in these different experiences of commonality. Explicit concern about what is common qua common depends on these first immersions and is linked to an implicit grasp of the varieties of commonality.

These varieties of being common help to tell us what common goods are and how we experience them. Central are goods that we can produce only in common—the beautiful symphony played by the orchestra, the team's victory. Some goods may also be enjoyed by those who do not help to produce them, paying spectators, say, or passersby on the outside. One may charge or penalize malingerers if one wishes. However, not only exercising one's powers in common, but also the spectator or subscriber's devotion to his own (i.e., what he loves), adds to the pleasure gained from the product simply and helps to explain actions such as voting or paying one's fair share.

Producing common goods also helps to explain justice and the place within common enterprises of separate members. Teams need their players to fit, which may not be equivalent to having the very best at each position when each is considered separately. Automobiles need to adjust engines, materials, brakes, and transmissions; they do not simply piece together the most powerful version of each. A beautiful face may not be comprised of the most beautiful eyes, lips, mouth, and so on, taken alone. Even in an orchestra, the best soloist may not be the best section leader. Nonetheless, when we properly adjust the best parts taken separately so they work with the others we might attain superior results.[9] The experience of participating in a common good of this orchestral sort is one of adjusting and limiting oneself as a part, combined with whatever expectations one has about one's own priority.[10]

What in these terms can we say about citizens in communities—about their differences in the same regime, as well as among different regimes? Citizenship, as Aristotle suggests, involves participation in ruling—in voting, jury service, and eligibility for legislative positions and magistracies. Not all members of communities are citizens. Some are resident aliens, some are deprived of citizenship, some are too young to be citizens. Slaves are not citizens, in many communities women are not citizens, and the criteria for citizenship exclude several men. This means that not all members of communities are equal. But does it suggest that citizens qua citizens are identical?

What differentiates various ways of life are the different goods to which they are directed and the distribution of tasks and opportunities connected to these goods. An understanding of how "I" differ from "us," how I strive for but am not identical to the excellence to which I can aspire, and how "we" (our city, country, or people) seek but differ from the justice of our regime simply also characterizes a way of life. This suggests that citizenship differs in different regimes. It also indicates that citizens within regimes may differ among themselves, namely, in relation to their contribution to producing and their ability to enjoy the defining goods, the defining goals, of the community. This difference in degrees of effective citizenship may be legal or customary, but it may also be factual because resources differ and permissible opportunities, skills, and activities produce different results. All citizens in the United States are equal, for example, but the very openness of our access to office favors the energetic, responsible, and well connected in fact.

So citizens in communities are not only similar as citizens—in elementary political participation—but also different, depending on the actual good that the common brings about. If countries must defend themselves, secure their independence, and provide necessities, and if they seek to produce a particular kind of happiness, excellence, or virtue, they must meet these functions. If these functions are met by different groups, the groups will be participating in producing the common goods—the security, provisions, and excellence that the members individually cannot produce—in different ways. Citizens experience the common differently when they are closer to or further from its distinctive purpose, the happiness or excellence toward which it is directed. As part of a common good directed toward ethical virtue, for example, economic matters and security will be subservient to and oriented to the ruling end. The citizens whose skills and efforts are closest to the goods that set the community's purpose— responsible freedom, righteousness, wealth, ethical virtue—are more fully citizens.[11] In traditional regimes, those closest both to the right path and to the divine origin are authoritative. In liberal democracies, the purpose is to secure equal rights, so citizenship is equal legally and in opportunity but, as I indicated, not in fact simply. Part of the strength of liberal democracy, however, part of common devotion to it, arises from this largely common experience of its goal. Equal citizenship in liberal democracy is found in equal access to its different tasks, in the equal accessibility of many of its distinctive virtues, and in the universality of its goal of securing rights.[12] But the factual differences in responsibility, talent, and luck give citizens unequal degrees of political control.

Political common goods are especially subtle because the parts that belong to the fullest end—freedom, virtue, or piety, for example— vary with ways of life.[13] Moreover, while not everyone on a team's roster is identical in contribution and enjoyment none is primarily ministerial, as some citizens may be, economically or militarily. Working through the subtleties of such political communities is the heart of Aristotle's *Politics*. The core issue is to understand virtue and why it is good.

THE LIBERAL DEMOCRATIC COMMUNITY

All political communities include some of the disparate functions I mentioned. But some communities are closer to being common in the sense of covering or joining what is identical. A clear example is our liberal democracy, where citizenship is not legally based on different contributions to the community or different ruling views of happiness but on equality in rights and criteria of membership such as birth. Factual differences exist in wealth, virtue, and talent, but a root equality in citizenship remains despite the greater effective power that belongs to some.

One reason root equality prevails is because, given the narrow view in liberal democracy of satisfaction as individual relief from unease, happiness does not in principle require a political community.[14] The common good, as representatives judge it, is what all such individuals would choose, given that choice without government—all life conducted as unregulated activity—leads to something none would choose. Politics is a necessary means in which the community's parts remain in principle identical "ones." Given equal access, I can improve myself justly only through free competition under laws. A certain set of virtues then also becomes necessary to secure the rights that allow satisfaction.

The narrowness of government in liberal democracy is evident in its distinction between state and society, where economic, intellectual, artistic, and religious life is primarily private and the state regulates or tries to ensure equal opportunity but does not direct it. Its central substantive political responsibilities are defense and public safety and, increasingly, assuring the education and economic standing that allow securing equal individual rights to be possible.

These limits to the purpose of politics and these restrictions in differences among citizens are visible in Hobbes and Locke and begin most clearly with Machiavelli's thought, where we can see the roots of the change from the classical view of the basic political phenomena and the way of life connected to them.[15] Enterprise and management in Machiavelli supplant classical statesmanship and do not apply only to politics narrowly conceived. The classical city or political community is replaced by the difference between state and society, and "states" need not be governments: governments are not politics' only or primary venue. Machiavellian virtue and prudence are not measures tied to specific goods and activities but, rather, are seen as characteristics, primarily bold cruelty and judgment, that one needs for success generally. Fortune or chance can be conquered through knowing and anticipating generally powerful motions and effects: chance is

not generally accepted as a consequence of the powers of specific unchanging things, as it is with the classics. To be excellent is not to be
guided by perfections one seeks to imitate, but by success one seeks
to emulate. The result, in relation to subsequent liberalism and liberal virtue, is the breadth, the lack of specific direction, of our virtues
and desires, the unity of our governmental powers and their separation from specific ends, the division of enterprise from attraction to
specific goods, and the split of government from religious orthodoxy.

I have discussed the importance of trust in practical activity, our
implicit and explicit expectations of what will happen next, and our
grasp of what happened before and of who will and should do what,
when. This trust differs in different activities, but the implicit general
understanding of what is permitted, of who can engage in activities
with what expected character or reliability, of how to persuade the
recalcitrant, and so on, is coherent in a regime and varies among them.
This variation is connected to how a regime is a whole, is something
common, for this indicates how its citizens fit as distinctive parts or,
rather, are equal and in principle identical. Most activities, however,
also have separate cosmopolitan meanings—directly as with the arts,
whose techniques are similar in different places, or as pointing to
more complete expressions in other regimes. Nonetheless, "I" first
experience this cosmopolitanism as part of a whole. Indeed, my experience of it may be largely absorbed in or occluded by our way and
traditions, especially when our way presents itself as the only way.

The Common Good and Patriotism

None of us is fully devoted to the common because we are also devoted to our own excellence and to what is our own simply. Indeed,
spiritedness and love show themselves even in the search for knowledge. Our good and my good are not identical, much as one might
attempt to make them so. Similarly, devotion to the common is not
only or usually to a way of life generally but to this way here and
now. My own, our own, our good, and my good differ.[16] To explore
what is common, therefore, we must say more about our connection

to this particular common good and not only to our way of life generally. I turn, therefore, to patriotism.

Patriotism is the political love of, the political attachment to, one's own. A "true" patriot is also loyal—steady and unwavering. Rather than attachment only to, say, liberal democracy, patriotism is attachment to America or Great Britain, this liberal democracy, or even this place whether or not it is democratic. The general concern with liberal freedom helps us to choose our allies, but it is not equivalent to our concern with ourselves. If our own liberal democracy were to slip away our effort to restore it would be greater than our effort to help others found their own. How, then, does patriotism work, and how is it connected to my other discussions?

I say "patriotism," because it is the most neutral indication for attachment to one's own country. As with other concepts, the neutral term or indication already has meaning derived from a specific context. We also talk of nationalism, one's ties to one's people, loyalty to the country, and now, indeed, to one's "identity"—one's people seen as a race or, perhaps, a religion or gender. The issue I will especially address is how much the experiences of freedom, justice, virtue, what is common, and the soul are tied not to one's regime or way generally but, rather, to one's particular country.

The object of patriotism, the country or city, seems to be a particular in relation to a general way of life: Great Britain, not liberal democracy generally. It is "particular" because it involves a particular place and time. But the place and time are not static. Patriotism's object is a particular but changing place (England, Great Britain, the United Kingdom) over a changing time historically. One way we consider this is to say that the regime is the form, the time and place are the matter, and the country or city (Athens) is the combination. Although any regime that actually forms a country will fall short of what is naturally best among regimes, we also sometimes think of the regime as the city's or country's nature, and its written and unwritten laws as its conventions, some more natural or connected to true justice than others.

The city or country, however, is not only our regime together with today's immediate or novel conventions. It is also what we have made and handed down. It is not simply a way of life in a given or variable place and time but also the accumulation of conventions and practices. It is not only these, moreover, but in countries such as ours it is also the accumulation of disputes about and extensions of our meaning—our historical "culture," as I have said—the differing and present understandings of our regime, of equality and liberty. Great Britain is a liberal democracy whose practices and conventions could in the extreme all leave the island and it would still be the same particular country in many or the most important respects. So the accumulation of practices and conventions belongs to the particular as much as do place and time, here and now, battles, and lists of kings and queens. Thus, in this view, I am loyal to, am patriotic about, a form of government, a way of life, an instance of justice or the common good but not only generally, as if I could be equally loyal to another liberal democracy (or tyranny). Rather, I am loyal (or perhaps no longer so loyal) to this instance of it, and what makes it particular is time and place and, also, practices, conventions, and the current and accumulated opinions about what the justice and goodness of our way of life now actually mean. Our "own" is the embodiment and projection of reason (form), opinions, practices, and place.

This combination and, especially, this place, moreover, are where my own usually (but not necessarily) resides: my property, my friends, my family. So patriotic loyalty is deepened to the extent that our home is my home: "national security" seeks to secure not only our way of life and practices, but our lives and property. Still, "our own" politically can never imitate altogether successfully the origin and separateness of the individual that it seeks to imitate. However much one sees "I" in terms of us, I can distinguish myself in thought, feeling, place, and time from our own in ways I cannot from my own. One can escape from one's country but not from oneself. True cosmopolitanism, however, is not relocation to another place and time physically or even imaginatively but, rather, openness in the ways I have discussed to varieties of justice and to the full correlates and objects of the individual soul.

Let me connect this view of patriotism with nationalism and develop my discussion. Nationalism suggests that the basis of politics is the nation. As with patriotism, it indicates birth and beginning, one's own, but it does so less directly because the patriot's fathers and founders are more visible and, indeed, more easily judged on the merits of their choices than is the more diffuse "nation" and its hazy spokesmen.

The "nation" is imprecisely defined, but it is a compound of ethnic, religious, and linguistic unity. And, in fact, no actual nation-state consists of a single nation. Rather than understanding the regime, the form of government, as what shapes or directs the differing conventions of people in different places, in nationalism the form of government is thought to be rightly chosen by the nation to suit its practices.[17] Some come to see self-determination as an element of liberal democracy, most obviously after the First World War, so that many expect nation-states sooner or later to become liberal democracies. But they need not, and in nineteenth-century nationalism this was not demanded. Within the particularity or reality of the nation, the regime is seen as only one fact among many. Indeed, the distinction between nature and convention, and form and matter, loses its force. The nation is the unity from which such distinctions might after the fact be made. This view differs from what I have just discussed — seeing the unity as a formed place, a country.

As nineteenth-century notions of history develop, the nation is seen primarily historically, in a manner that is related to the historical variation and accumulation of drives that Nietzsche discusses which connects a type of race and even gender to history. The proper political home for Nietzsche's superman, however, is not the single nation but united Europe.[18] In Hegel, a people is unfinished but in a historically progressive way that may ultimately complete it.

The nation, seen primarily as an ethnicity or race that can be directed to illiberal as well as liberal politics, dominates political discussion from nineteenth-century imperialism until the beginning of the Second World War. A powerful example is Heidegger, who, as I said, thinks of authentic politics primarily in terms of the people, the political analogue to the authentic individual (authentic *Dasein*), with an emphasis on essential moods and unity, and where race and space are significant not as physical or biological causes but as factors made meaningful when they are taken up into a people's pursuit of its possibilities.[19]

Such a people differs from the liberal people John Locke has in mind, or our American "we the people," who are essentially self-chosen and gathered: a people is any group that chooses to place itself under a common authority based on principles such as those of the Declaration of Independence, whatever the considerable importance of preexisting ties. The distinction between the natural and the particular or conventional that is visible in the liberal view of a people and in liberal patriotism is unavailable or overwhelmed in the ethnic-nationalist conception and Heidegger's version of it. The effect in Heidegger's case is to attempt to unify all the people's activities so that each loses its independent or cosmopolitan status.[20]

The failure or extremism of this conception shows that our activities within a nation, country, city, or homeland cannot be encompassed fully by the "people" or by any group identity and that the inescapable individual is not mirrored by an inescapable people or public. This is apparent in liberal republics, and also in classical Greek cities, especially democracies or mixed regimes.[21] Our people and its government are in fact not the only authority. We require a community if we are to experience any higher possibilities of art, thought, and statesmanship, but it need not be this one precisely. We are embedded in a particular country, but this embeddedness exists in a circle that opens up and out to questions of truer justice and excellence. We are immersed in the natural as well as the conventional, and we may free ourselves individually and improve ourselves politically.[22]

The variety of ways to grasp the connection and separation of the general and the particular stems from our experience within a community that is similar to others of its type but that, nonetheless, because of friendship, love, familiarity, conventions, culture, trust, enjoyment, and the necessities of production, becomes the object of one's patriotism.[23] Differences can then always appear between one's own way and what is truer, better, and more just, as deliberation and opinion can lead one to this. An inevitable openness to reason exists.

Perhaps the exception to what I have just claimed is the close tie between the good and one's own in a strictly traditional or religious way of life. In a sense, the notion of nations and ethnic peoples is a return to this view, after distinctions have been made between our way, the just way, and good ways. For in communities where our way is the good or proper way because of a divine beginning and guidance, we live prior to such explicit distinctions. Whether in such communities one can fully do without some understanding of the difference between my pleasure and wishes and the community's demands, or between claims some make through dreams or prophesy to direct contact with gods and what is publicly visible, may seem unclear. I indicated earlier why this is unlikely. In any event, the taken for granted or attempted identity between our laws and what is good and just shows us how noticing these distinctions is central for thought and how splits between one's own good (or pleasure) and the righteous way, and between private and publicly visible knowledge, indicate the imperfections that can spur further reflection, even in the most closed community. The truncating of human powers in such communities will result in misdirected spiritedness and unfulfilled desires.[24]

PATRIOTISM AND THE BODY

I have argued that the soul, not the body, is central to identity and that patriotism concerns the way of life, the changing "cultural" understanding of its meaning, and one's familiar conventions and practices more than it does the land alone. Nonetheless, patriotism also involves land and resources. How important, then, is the body—both our or my particular body—individually and politically? "How important" means for understanding what we are, how we are, and what happiness is.

The body is especially significant as a beginning point for what is formed by motive and direction, by meaning. Discussions about founding cities or countries involve among other matters the best material situation: what size, proximity to the sea, and resources are most favorable? They also involve other issues, of course, including the expectations and opinions of the people one is forming. And the chief question even concerning land is the way of life that one is attempting to institute.[25]

The reasons these material issues matter is because they help to provide limits to what a community can do militarily and economically. They are also important because they help to set the original expectations for the community: will it be largely self-sufficient, is its military effort primarily on land or sea, does it harbor wishes for expansion into territories it considers to be unformed? The meaning and experience of the country is primarily in terms of its practices, conventions, and way of life, but these are limited by place and resources and are experienced "here" rather than somewhere else. Loyalty politically is not often to a place alone and as such, but it is rarely apart from it. One is attached to this country as ours to rule.

These limits, thus, are a significant element in our political excellence and freedom. The spiritedness, pride, and courage that motivate our freedom and defend our common activity always exist together with and to a degree are for and about this place, now. And this place now involves how we began and, also, what we have accumulated. Similarly, excellence, improvement, and justice politically have their initial and some of their ongoing direction restricted by how we begin and what we have accumulated. This involves place and resources— property. One's own resources are needed for one's way of life and for the pride and freedom of self-government. Moreover, one requires a certain degree of continuity for free and just action, hence a degree of continuity in the country's "body." Thus there is likely to be a decline if one separates the country too much from this continuity.

THE BODY AND THE INDIVIDUAL

It is not only our territory and resources that change, for I can leave a political body individually. How easy or permissible this is depends on ways of life: as I have said, the political body has its effect and meaning primarily in terms of the way of life and the directions it gives. But one cannot simply leave one's own body, if one can leave it at all.

I am arguing that our meaning as bodily depends primarily on eros and spiritedness and how the independence experienced in their movements is understood and developed within a way of life. But I should also remark on the limits or directions to meaning that one's body itself sets. For the initial experience of one's own as enclosed and the initial experience of oneself as open involve the body and the senses. We cannot separate what we enjoy from its highest or purest goal, but we also cannot separate it altogether from its ordinary sensory reflections, or from what we possess. Desires reflect and ultimately seek the beauty and knowledge that are not sensual. But they are always influenced by the original experience of these goods that is inseparable from one's own body. Virtue, for example, requires continuity and integrity of the body: it requires longevity, loyalty, and attachment. Indeed, one needs a healthy body and sufficient resources for proper enjoyment. But virtue itself shows that we are basically formed by the experience of reasonable eros and spiritedness.

The connection of goods to original experiences that one can hardly separate from one's body is also relevant for considering the status of the apparent universality of some bodily facts among human beings. Different ways of life see these somewhat differently, but common facts and functions exist in all—childbirth, the need to educate the young, the presence of death, and the facing of possible hunger and illness. Even when we limit poor health and poverty in much of modernity, we must still understand what we are trying to overcome.

These facts are significant for how we form expectations and for understanding how meaningful things are first reflected in the senses. They are basic for the goods and happiness we later seek and for the development and direction of our eros and pride. Love and child-rearing, for example, affect our subsequent direction. Yet not only today's technology and range of choice, but even a work as early as Plato's *Republic* shows how complicated and variable this apparently simple natural beginning is. After all, Plato's best regime equates men and women and treats reproduction and child-rearing from the perspective of what seems most useful politically. Nonetheless, this regime is not possible in the flesh, and both Plato's *Laws* and Aristotle's *Politics* indicate that, whatever the possibilities legally and technically, the natural family is still central for the first step toward human excellence.[26] Bodily differences that are significant in the family are implicated in the direction and degree of eros and spiritedness that are central for the freedoms we defend and the satisfactions we seek.

Our first loving aspiration is to elevate ourselves to another, or to be together with them and then be attached to what is joint, the child. This aspiration and attachment are to another soul, but as it informs this body. This first openness and loyalty, this first combining of man, woman, and child, is crucial as the ground for other openness, however much the development of the I, the separateness of the couple, or the direction of further excellence depends on one's overall way of life. One can never simply change this beginning: later choice will always be based to a degree on what already has happened because eros and spiritedness love and protect in relation to specific things, even if there are higher things.

Infinite reshaping of the body is thus not possible without goods being given up, restricted, or distorted—love, loyalty, family, and freedom in various venues—that we also need for what is higher and more complete. Attempting to bypass the body will have real although not simply predictable results: good things of the senses as well as love and loyalty will be at risk. As I indicated in my discussion of the limits to what technology can accomplish, and as one sees in the mistakes of radical attempts that try to equate the good and one's own, certain things cannot be brought about whatever the effort, and much will be lost and distorted when impossible or excessive change is attempted.[27] Trust, expectations, and the steadiness we need for openness will also be harmed by such attempts.

In the last analysis, we cannot change the meaning of things. But our aspirations and understanding will be affected by ignoring this truth. Our guidance depends on what is good, and goods are first reflected in and motivate us within our initial natural attachments.[28] The issue is what will be restricted in our aspirations, freedom, and pride by the attempt to completely master and reform our body.[29]

Chapter Six

The Nature of Goods

Politics and justice concern the common good. While we might agree that we can understand how we produce or enjoy some things only in common, the question of what actually is good seems difficult to resolve. After all, scholars have claimed for centuries that what ought to be cannot be derived from what is (although both "are") or that what is good is a value that we cannot show to exist beyond its being desired or powerfully asserted. What is good is what we want or can impose, and this differs among us.

By contrast, I argue that we can discuss what is good reasonably. But we must also account for why it is so disputed.

The phenomenon of doing what is best appears preconceptually. Anything we do is to be done well, or in the right way. Perhaps we do not always distinguish what is good from the right or righteous (or the gods') way, but ordinary success or failure in a hunt or in growing food will be clear. Indeed, success and failure are often attributed to the gods, so we see them, too, in relation to what is good. One's own good may not be distinguished clearly from "our" good, but what is better or more successful could always be discriminated. Nonetheless, despite this pre-philosophical evidence for much that is good or better, we must also see how and why what is good is so often disputed—why it is disputable.

The Uses of "Good"

Let us consider various uses of "good." What is a good path to victory? What is a good (or the best) dish to order here? This is a *good* meal. What would a good outcome be? What would be the very best result? What is best, given the circumstances? What course of study is it good for me to pursue? This symphony is very good. This is a very good car. This is an excellent car. This is a good job for you. This is a good hammer. That effort is good enough. He is a good man. He is a good musician. She is not just a good violinist but a great one. Good dog! He is a good teammate. This is a good temperature. Good day! This is a good fit. This is a very good fit. This is an excellent fit. This is a perfect fit. That's good; it couldn't be better. She is in a good mood. Goods and services. Household goods.

When we consider these uses we see that what is good involves several general characteristics. It guides actions: one asks what a good path to victory is, what a good or the best dish to order is in a restaurant, or what a good fit might be. It is an action's chief purpose, end, or measure: one asks what a good outcome or result is, or what actually counts as victory. It is choiceworthy: one asks what course of study it is good to pursue. It is something's working or functioning at a high or full level, as a good brain works well, as someone has good practical sense, or as a healthy body is better than an unhealthy one. It is something's perfection: one says that a symphony is very good—truly excellent—or that something is a good fit and could not be better. (It lacks nothing, and possesses everything that belongs to it.) In this regard, when we say, "*That* was a meal," symphony, game, and so on, we are suggesting that the true or complete instances of something are its better or best instances, those on which we could not improve.

What is good is also serviceable or useful: one knows that this hammer is a good one. It is also what is adequate, sufficient, or beneficial without needing to be excellent, as is a good house or job "for you." It can be a general characteristic that colors other activities, as a good teammate fits in generally or considers the team as a whole, or a good man is decent, thoughtful, and responsible, that is, has a good character or is virtuous.

As an end or goal, what is good completes or satisfies rather than merely stopping or being over. It allows things to be and be known, as we see in Plato's *Republic*: desiring a good chair, say, is a goal that brings about the acts (the "measures") that produce it and allow them to be seen as such. What is good or satisfactory, however, is not quite what is very good, excellent, or the best. What is very good is really or truly good, fully useful or complete, lacking nothing and possessing everything that belongs to its kind. It is exemplary, excellent, perfect, and, therefore, choiceworthy or guiding. In a more ordinary sense it is satisfactory and also choiceworthy or guiding. So, in the fullest sense, what is good is what is complete, choiceworthy, and guiding and, therefore, the source from which we judge adequate results and useful measures and means.

This account of what is good may seem inadvertently to cover what is not "good"—the perfect crime, say. How can we distinguish here? Three points are significant: understanding the full or complete use of something's powers; understanding how things and actions fit within communities or wholes; and understanding a particular end's connection to other ends, such as pleasure. The perfect crime does not use our full powers, it harms others' goods excessively, and it is unlikely to achieve the full pleasure that is one of its goals, let alone satisfy still other ends. In other words, what seems good as complete or perfect in a particular respect is seldom independent but, rather, points to what is more full, or even, altogether complete. When Plato and Aristotle claim that the philosophical life is best they mean that it uses all our human powers most completely, is oriented directly to the unchanging whole without detracting from others, and is pleasant. When one claims that a statesman's life or a life of ethical virtue is excellent or best one means that it is a full if not altogether complete and pleasant use of our powers that also aids others' excellence in a common enterprise, even though statesmanship is not directed to the whole simply, as philosophers seek to understand it.[1]

WHY IS WHAT IS GOOD DISPUTED?

If matters are so simple, why is the question of what is good, or how best to live, so disputed? One reason for dispute is the evident inequality in the view I am presenting, a difficulty especially salient today, if not always, given our dislike of calling anything inherently better than anything else, a dislike connected to our basis in equal natural rights. A second reason for dispute is the complexity of human freedom and individuality, which means that my happiness depends on using and therefore possibly misusing my own likely inferior powers. (As I have said, attachment to my own, our own, what is good, and what is just often differ.) A third reason for dispute about what is good is speech itself, which often allows fraud to triumph. A fourth is the importance of pleasure in what is good and the complexity of pleasure's elements and sources. A fifth reason for dispute about the good is the scarcity of so many resources required to enjoy what is good, and the significance of strength or force. A sixth is the possibility that we might doubt, question, or rebel against the power, attraction, and natural guidance of completion and perfection. (As I have said, all seemingly can be overcome.) A seventh, connected to these points, is what I have discussed as the variety of ways good things first approach us, the various notions of goodness. Each way of life first projects and takes for granted a certain understanding, although the views in the different regimes are linked. An eighth cause of dispute is the difficulty of measuring excellence because matters are so complex and different goods may be or seem incommensurable.

PLEASURE AND EQUALITY

Let me develop this discussion. Good things approach us within our way of life, and, therefore, we favor or disfavor certain practices and activities. What is considered to be just co-directs the appearance of what is good. Physical pleasure, for example, is an obvious incentive for individuals to stray from the righteous path, or conceive themselves as separate from the community. It is, therefore, especially condemned or manipulated in theocracies so that enjoying individual pleasure is divorced from what is done appropriately. Yet physical pleasure cannot help but be attractive. The result of the condemnation together with the hidden attraction is that we can miss the link between pleasure and virtuous action, can overlook the subtle varieties of pleasure, and can overlook virtues such as moderation or reduce them to following the (religious) law. This distortion of pleasure through the emphasis on one type of pleasure and condemning it obfuscates what is good generally, its attraction, and the natural orientation of justice to it. For good things as attractive are never wholly separate from pleasure.[2] Understanding what is good becomes difficult from the standpoint that separates the pleasant and the good.

The revolt against subjugating pleasure also distorts pleasure. If one considers the modern revolution against priestly control, the consequent liberating of human energies, and the attempt to master or redirect nature, one sees that it is connected to a particular view of pleasure—pleasure as relief from unease, on the model of physical pleasure but even more neutral than the filling of specific emptiness. So all goods are seen to approach us equally as pleasure, pleasures are not distinguished according to their origin, and we do not take notions of fulfillment seriously when we devote ourselves to restless accumulation. Entrepreneurial (or "princely") efforts to overcome natural limits in order to expand the resources for pleasure become vital. This orientation also has the effect of making particular ends with a visible universal base—health and comfort—come to the fore.

Even within this simple standpoint of pleasure as relief from unease, however, complexity about what is good and, especially, about common goods emerges. Goods are largely commensurable in liberal democracies' view of goodness as relief from unease because they are equated and measured in terms of "added" pleasure. But the enjoyers of goods are those with rights. They therefore have separate claims to a degree of inviolability. As I have discussed, one cannot properly punish or take unjustly to bring about a greater total of social or others' pleasure. Still, there is no simple or correct answer to what is just in each and every situation when the common good and individual rights clash, let alone when one tries to differentiate pleasures so that the source or experience of some (poetry, say) counts for more than others (pinball, say).

Natural goods and pleasure are related in still more complex ways. Virtue's connection to pleasure is not limited to moderately controlling sensual pleasure. For pleasure can involve seeing, observing, thinking, and knowing and not only what is physical. Moreover,

pleasure is not only filling an emptiness or lack. It can be an expanding, swelling, burgeoning, swooning, or intensifying, as when one
hears or sees something beautiful, exquisite, or refined.[3] Even experiencing physical pleasure involves knowing and discriminating, and
seeing someone beautiful is pleasant even though one experiences no
previous lack or unease. Indeed, each virtuous act—doing what is
beautiful—is pleasant. So the pleasures of different activities cannot
simply be stripped from them and added up because of the variety of
experiences involved in them, even those that are primarily sensed.[4]
Some pleasures may come at another's expense or together with
others, moreover, making pleasures still more difficult to compare,
rank, and measure. This difficulty is exacerbated by the fact that some
pleasures may be calm, gentle, or even almost indifferent, as in thinking or in experiencing what is pure and unmixed.

These varieties of pleasure are tied to particular activities and
fulfillments and to the rank of these activities. But the activities are
not ranked by pleasure alone, which does not in all respects increase
with increased activity: too much of some pleasures might be cloying, so that more is not always more pleasant. In short, the complexity
of pleasure makes choice, especially common choice, difficult. One
strength of liberal democracy is that publicly focusing on securing
equal rights and, therefore, on the principle of equality of pleasures is
(often) the least contentious practice.

A related problem that makes choice contentious is that regimes
based on equal rights, and, perhaps, some ways of life that involve
walking the righteous path, are unlikely to defend or support inequality. They will allow or practice it for priests and for the wealthy
who (can be said to) provide goods useful for all but who do not (in
the case of the wealthy) lead a way of life markedly different from the
rest of us. If there is no public justification for excellent or exceptional
powers fully used, however, it can be difficult for these to flourish. In
any event, what is "good" is the proper way or, in liberal democracy,
the pleasure you choose, not what is closer to a standard of our
powers' full use. This standard cannot be fully hidden, of course, because it is natural, and one will see its images when we are encouraged
to do what the community thinks best, encouraged by parents or, in

the now somewhat older view, asked to do the best we can with our talents.[5] Nonetheless, the impetus is strong against arguing that something is a better or more complete end than another. One reason what is good is disputed is because what is best is hidden, and one reason it is hidden is because of the dislike of inequality, perhaps, especially, natural inequality.

FREEDOM

Still another, related, difficulty is the status and complexity of human freedom. Because we are free, we are free to ignore, reject, and make mistakes. But we cannot enjoy properly without exercising reason, or engaging in reason's forming of desire, spiritedness, and our passions. Attempts to live a life that ignores reason—drugs, alcohol, sloth—ignore our powers and fall short of satisfying them.[6]

Here, the point is that it is not always easy for individuals freely to acknowledge what is better, to and for themselves. Freedom protects itself, it protects one's own, through stubbornness and pride. It protects itself as well by the desire to do things for oneself, if not all things, many. There is always some discrepancy between one's own and the good, between recognizing what is best and doing things oneself but less well. This discrepancy is connected to (but is not identical to) the fact that even with people's open acknowledgment of excellence and ranks they will still see matters differently from each other because of differences in their own powers and circumstances. Free ordering of passions will lead us to judge and desire differently, our varied circumstances will do so, too, and protecting our freedom will lead to stubborn recalcitrance to bow simply, even to what is or seems true. So our freedom and being our own mean that what we each see as good will sometimes look different among us, even with reasonable intentions. Moreover, it will often in fact be and not merely seem different because what is good for me will not be the best simply. Not all resources will go to those who might use them best because each also wants them to be used for his own good. To the degree that my freedom is itself a good, and to the degree that this is true generally, what is simply good for me and us will be disputed.

Scarce Resources

A further difficulty that leads to dispute about what is good is scarcity of resources. This makes enjoying goods limited and competitive, so actions seem better or worse depending on whether scarcity and inequality appear desirable or not. The possibilities for fully using one's powers in relation to the most complete goods are limited. There are only so many opportunities for rule or for magnificent spending. This scarcity may seem especially attractive when restricted competition exists and when goods present themselves beautifully or perfectly. When the standpoint is more egalitarian, however, such scarcity may seem undesirable, especially when what is good presents itself as relief from unease. Overcoming scarcity—but with controlled or limited competition of our American sort—then seems desirable. (Love is still another good that can be competitive, moreover—although we are told there is someone for everyone.) The philosophical life is another "solution" to the dialectic of scarcity and equality by being both rare and not rare: it is open to those few who have the requisite ability, but there is no scarcity of what is available to know. The point here is that these issues of scarcity and equality can block what is good from view, and further block it through dispute.

Lying and Questionability

Still another fact distorts our view of what is good, namely, the ability to lie or "persuade" that is true speech or reason's twin. It seems surprisingly easy to convince people to renounce ordinary goods or pleasures in search of promised remote purity or never-ending pleasure, or to engage in destruction. The history of religious obsession and political terror makes this clear. (One may believe in one's own religion, but one doubts the others.) The cause can be hope, fear, incompetence, or the inability to question in the face of tradition and community. The point is that we can manipulate views of proper or acceptable lives, or of the reasonable range of violence and force. Lies may even be caused by necessity. Indeed, many divergent views are partially true, as we see with everyday opinions or in Plato's dialogues. We might even say that we begin by being immersed in opinion and error, not altogether, perhaps, but substantially. The result, again, is that access to reasonable or adequate views of what is good and just is available but occluded or blocked.

Still another reason we dispute what is good is that the issues I am discussing are never simply resolved, so awareness of them as questions remains. Indeed, serious incompatibility exists among several activities that use our abilities and are pleasurable. Philosophically calling important matters into question may affect the useful security of following reigning expectations and opinions. Spirited and responsible political and economic activity disrupt short-term calm. One might suggest, as Plato does, that the fullest eros is in the philosophical love of the beautiful, but this love still differs in pleasure, intensity, and the sensual from art and sex. As I have suggested, courage of the intellect is like but different from a warrior's courage. To the degree that using our powers means or requires questioning and exploration, fundamental questions will always present themselves, so simple agreement will not occur, even if practical agreement is possible, for a while.

The most telling, if not the most profound, difficulty in agreeing on or simply measuring what is good, even if one can rank ways of life and good things generally, is, as I have said, visible in the difference between respecting equal rights and seeking what is good. It is the most telling because in trying to overcome this difference one comes closest to attempting to bring together coherently what is always to some degree incompatible—what is good, one's own, our own, and what is just.[7]

THE GOODNESS OF WAYS OF LIFE

I should also discuss the difficulties that arise from how goods first present themselves as good. The contexts and expectations in which we are first immersed concern activities we believe to be proper, acceptable, fitting, and the opposite, and particular things we believe to be good or desirable: we are involved with an implicit grasp of what is fitting and of what we can do with ourselves and others.[8] These actions and goods will first approach us primarily in regime-related ways. I say "primarily," because each understanding of justice is open to the others, and several goods have a character that will look similar, however transformed by a way of life. The meaning and choiceworthiness of health or victory, the differences among men, women, and children, or the utility of plants and animals (for food, say) will have some identity of powers in any human context. Still, even here, one recognizes the degree of human variety, so that some plants are not considered for cultivation, some animals are treated as sacred, we do not always do what we must to prepare for victory, health is not everywhere identically ranked in relation to other goods, and the freedoms given women or the age of maturity for children vary widely. Understanding the degree of what is identical and what is not in the different common experiences of what is good is difficult. Moreover, as I have said, what is nearly identical about things across ways of life may often not be what is most important about them. In any event, most matters of character and the choice and desirability of activities approach us in terms of our ways of life. The variety in understanding the goodness of goods and the different kinds of commonality in common goods adds to the difficulty of judging what is good, and helps to constitute its disputability.

I have discussed the modern liberal democratic way in which all goods approach us as equally choosable objects of desire, where desire is unease that they can relieve. This view coheres with equal rights, the trust, expectations, and common sense (which always are to some degree "culturally" changing) that enable us to go about our activities, the modern virtues or character that we cultivate, limited or merely ministerial government, and an equalizing of pleasures. Other approaches do not become impossible: when we choose activities from within what "we" first believe can be good we may address them in ways that lead to other directions. This is especially so in contemporary liberalism and enhances our complexity. Still, our first, given, "traditional" understanding is our market or technological view.

The existence of other presentations within and before liberalism complicate how things can first seem good and, therefore, what appears good concretely. Hence, we face still another difficulty in seeing what is desirable, let alone in reaching agreement. I have discussed the view (which I am largely presenting as the origin from which the others develop or decline) through which what is guiding and choice-worthy offers itself in the deepest sense as complete, noble, rare, and exclusive and what contributes to this, one in which good things are things as a noble or virtuous character experiences them and as they are connected to a classical notion of the soul's powers and movements. Coordinated with this standpoint is a fuller sense of pleasure and satisfaction than we see in liberal democracies and restrictions on using property and on the availability of political offices. Land is still land, but we do not treat or experience it as something to buy and sell neutrally.

In each case, our human choice starts within a form of justice, a presentation of what can be good, and our correlated character-istics. This implicitly opens to the truly just and good and the full use of our characteristics, together with a correlated separating of one's own pride and inviolability, and some inevitable particularity of one's "people." Necessities that are more or less universal stand within regimes, so that they are often met and understood with different degrees of urgency in different ways of life.

An understanding of the centrality of noble action and the importance of virtue may seem basically aristocratic. Still, classical democracies also are restricted in citizenship: their principle of freedom is an openness to equal satisfaction based on different pleasures as filling different desires. They are not based on transforming nature, on limiting government, on radically expanding wealth, or on the equivalence of pleasures as relief from unease. Classical democracies are connected as well to courage, moderation, and appropriate generosity, and to honesty and friendliness. Nonetheless, there is a likeness between ancient and modern freedom because of equality in liberty and the significance of desire.

OTHER VIEWS OF GOODS' COMPLEXITY

I should also mention here other views about the variability of what is good. In Hegel's understanding, what seems choiceworthy today is in fact always a way station to a practical and philosophical perfection that brings together all goods. Each major choice—of property, contracts, punishment, morality, family, professional and political life—believes itself to be sufficient or satisfactory but is in fact only a step on the path to the conclusion of the course. What occurs is not an image of what is ahistorically whole but a necessary part or element (that mistakenly believes itself whole) in a path to the completed end.

Despite Hegel's arguments, however, one may wonder whether the final point can in fact overcome the divisions among the experiences of my own freedom and its best use, of self-government and good government, and of thought and faith. In some ways, this difficulty is the basis of Kierkegaard's and Nietzsche's criticisms of Hegel. In Nietzsche, to go beyond good and evil is first to reach back to what is aristocratically good and bad. What is good, however, is ultimately not what is aristocratic alone but what comes to light as expressing the command and overcoming of the superman, primarily his internal command and overcoming. What is good can be seen in terms of a human project (the superman) who confidently fixes in place but then upends any previously settled human perspective. He works with the history, the fate, of previous human creating and establishing—morality, religion, thought, and art—and grounds himself on the drives and human types so created. Unlike Nietzsche, however, previous "discoverers" of standards of what is good did not understand their own arbitrariness or their creative beginning as expressions of power.

The similarities (but, of course, not identity) between Nietzsche's superman and classical philosophical virtue—the philosopher as commander and legislator or as erotic-spirited knower—allow comparison of Nietzsche's claims and other ways of life and theoretical arguments. This is also true, as I suggested, with similarities between classical and modern democracies. As I have argued, modern thinkers

do not in fact discover new human phenomena. Nor can they invent
any that are fundamentally significant. The place to begin to assess
this claim is the classical standpoint, as one has worked back to it from
our own standpoint.[9]

Measuring What Is Good

Let me conclude this consideration of what is good by examining
further the possibility of commensurability and measurement.[10] The
issues we are considering help to make clear why what is good for
human beings is disputable. They point to the difficulty of choosing
definitively, either individually or as a community, among ways of
life, among the goods toward which they are directed, and among the
virtues and moral actions that limit these goods.

Nonetheless, the issues I am discussing also allow us to see how
in principle we can judge these disputes: guidelines for measuring and
judging do exist, and I have indicated several. Such measuring is not
calculating but, rather, seeing wholes and parts in their complexity
and comprehensiveness: it is noetic and discursive. The most basic criterion is the fullest use of our powers, primarily speech or reason, but
also the reasoned experience of passions and ordinary goods. Such
intellectual and ethical virtue is grounded on the experiences of recognizing what it is to speak truly, and to use ordinary goods well.
(This criterion is not merely a matter of opinion, although employing
it is subtle.) Moreover, even as new modes of enjoyment and art
become available, these criteria remain powerful. They allow us to
note what is intellectually too narrow or pointless, what restricts and
distorts the experience of the beautiful and the honorable, and what
unduly constrains or fails to direct the senses. This use of our powers,
moreover, is accompanied by pleasure, once pleasure is understood in
the full range of its elements and the activities it accompanies. For we
are concerned not only with using our powers but also with what is
pleasant in them.

This general standard, largely developed at the beginning of
thought, then also allows us to judge how best to use different degrees
of our powers in different circumstances, and which circumstances to

seek. Mediocre art is less noble than loving friendship and reasonable generosity. Exercising one's virtue and prudence is generally more important than being bound to a lucrative but mechanical job. The grounds of these judgments are not calculation but, rather, looking at, considering, the fit and elevation of one's powers and enjoyments within a just whole.

This standard is both advanced and complicated by one's pride in self-direction, by spirited self-defense and protecting some level of individual inviolability and fair treatment. Goods must always be good as one's own, experienced together with one's own effort and choice. They cannot display their power simply alone and apart. But this does not guarantee that one chooses well or as is necessary politically. The central element that makes proper choice more likely is education to liberate the widest freedom and to direct us to what is intellectually and ethically virtuous. If the standard is the excellent use of our powers and the relevant pleasures, together with respect for our pride and inviolability—equal rights—we must teach the proper ground for recognizing both rights and excellence. Each good one seeks, however independent, must also become one's own, one's possession, yet never simply this.

The higher goods require leisure. We have a good degree of that. The reasons that purported to justify slavery in the past do not exist now. The issue for us today is the flattening and forgetting of excellence. But communities that are or claim to be aristocratic (or religiously aristocratic) will likely be fraudulent and need not be risked. This includes our own movement to an aristocracy of wealth and wasted talent. The grounds on which one presses oneself forward most fully—the openness to excellence, and pride—do not distinguish oneself and one's class alone.

This points to still another element of proper measure, namely, the need to preserve the ordinary venues and experiences of excellence—family, friendship, everyday trust, the relations between men and women. Certain goods, perhaps especially love and friendship but also education, require a stable background that recognizes the appropriate beginnings for forming one's expectations and directing one's activities. These beginning limits are a source, but not the only source, of using one's natural talents and desires well.

It is also true, as I have said, that modern versions of Aristotle's virtues exist. Toleration, industriousness, and civility are coordinate with equality in rights and the consequences of a regime based on them. Responsibility works from this ground but opens to a fuller impressing of one's freedom. It also allows the classical virtues to flourish but within the atmosphere of equality.

The practical "solution" to the problem of choosing goods is, therefore, threefold: first, individually, the fullest or most virtuous use of our powers and the education that allows and develops this; second, basing this use and education on the natural meaning of trust, love, family, friendship, and limits in resources; and, third, doing this in a community grounded on equal individual choice and pride, on trust whose expectations rest on these virtues and meaning and on understanding our powers and their truly excellent use. Here, what is central is the possibility of questioning, of rising beyond the ways and activities in which one is engaged, while recognizing the basic agreement and trust in which exploration and improvement must be embedded. We usually consider most of our activities only up to a point, one of the many reasons it is better to be in a place formed by a good way than a bad one. But it is best if room exists for elevation together with modesty about the complexity of choice, and understanding of the power of pride as well as of attraction. The disappointments, distortions, and difficulties in communities that attempt to combine the aristocratic and democratic are inevitable but controllable. Such combining does have the effect of limiting full political pride. But the reasonable substitute is responsibility and entrepreneurial activity. It also has the effect, for now, of reducing the public impact of the excellent—but not necessarily the private impact—and of increasing narrowness and specialization. Against this one must secure the possibility of intelligent public agreement, and cosmopolitan breadth.

Do Our Standards Still Guide When Our Powers Appear to Change?

One might ask how the standards I have discussed could help us decide what is good or what happiness is if we are capable of changing ourselves radically. These standards are based on using our powers fully in relation to passions we experience and satisfactions we seek. But if we are seemingly capable of changing our basic characteristics, what guidance could they offer? Indeed, what guidance could they offer for understanding and directing artificial intelligences—or for their own self-direction?

I will discuss several issues. One is that we are asking this question, now. That is to say that it is intelligible in terms of our capabilities today, even as we can see ourselves expanding or perhaps narrowing our capabilities tomorrow. So our questions and answers now will and must be meaningful in our present terms, both for our immediate concerns and more fundamentally.

By immediate concerns I have in mind the link between freedom, warfare, and technology.[11] This link makes it dangerous to limit technology in our country or in liberal democracies generally when other countries and regimes may not restrict their efforts.[12] This tie remains a significant practical reason why the kinds of work that gave us guns, airplanes, radar, and atomic weaponry cannot be reduced while competitive political regimes exist, as they do now and will continue to in the future. The fact that such efforts may today involve changes or extensions of our own capabilities, with the attendant risks, does not, practically, eliminate political danger. Efforts to restrict the use of various technologies internationally are important, and our fears of what they might bring about are real, but to fall behind is to risk political and then individual freedom. The basic arguments and considerations here are not new and have been especially salient for the past seventy-five years.

More fundamentally, the question involves the relevance and truth in the future of the grounds and standards of what is good for us now and the degree to which they could be overcome for better or, practically, for worse. Yet in terms of what, precisely, would ethical virtue and intellectual virtue be overcome properly? Ethical virtue involves having and employing fitting dispositions for enjoying and governing goods and passions. Could this change radically? Would the measure of what is proper change or only what, say, is concretely moderate or courageous in new situations? Could some of the virtues vary fundamentally if the goods with which they deal no longer seem choiceworthy? The inherent limits to enjoying some goods, which I just discussed, and the inherent limits to physical causes and conditions that I mentioned in my examination of freedom will not change. It could be that the attractiveness of some goods will diminish or, perhaps, be enhanced as technology lengthens life spans or the character of the family changes. One could not predict with precision the results of such occurrences. But such variation would not alter the basic standpoint of proper choice. Rather, it might affect what choices actually count as moderate, as proper anger, as courageous, and so on, or even diminish and perhaps seem to eliminate the possibilities for magnificence and greatness of soul. But should this occur it will not alter the standards themselves.

This would also be true of intellectual virtue. It would be difficult to argue that the mind should not be enhanced, if not for oneself, but for those one loves. The meaning of truth will not change, however. Nor would the mind's fullest use.

Can one defend not only the proper use of the passions and mind, but their very existence? If the mind properly used is not good, however—that is, if it is not something that guides and satisfies and helps bring out the intelligibility of other actions—what else could be? How would the question of choice even be relevant or intelligible?

Is this link between the mind and what is choiceworthy also true of our passions and the goods with which they deal? If only a restricted or nonexistent eros exists in the future we would have narrow aspirations and, presumably, diminished transcending outside and beyond ourselves. A restriction would also exist in what we could experience. One might imagine an unlikely world of pure intellectual understanding without the effort of search but perhaps restricted by the inability to grasp bodily things, their powers, and the link of these powers to what we can understand in its purity. Or if eros existed but only in some truncated manner, we might experience the irresponsibility of Greek gods and goddesses or the continued decline of eros to mere desire. On the whole, the existence and virtuous direction of eros would seem to be necessary for proper aspiration and experience.

Without it, artistic creation would also diminish, even if becoming more widespread, through lack of serious subjects and motives.

If in the future there would be only restricted or nonexistent spiritedness, moreover, one might wonder how we could defend equal freedom, for this depends on the presence of spiritedness and its not declining, or declining further. One would wonder as well how the pride that seems necessary for energy and aspiration would exist. We have already seen the diminishing of great pride and, perhaps, magnificence. But this has proved consonant with equal freedom, and diminished spiritedness is not its disappearance: responsibility has proved for now to be a reasonable substitute, which, properly understood, should help to preserve the pride that works against spiritedness's further diminution. It may decline on its own, just as eros may, but this would be undesirable.[13]

The key point is that happiness or what is good could not properly change for intellectual beings unless passions and the mind changed unimaginably. The net effect of what I am arguing is that our present standards should continue to guide future acts, however unpredictable some elements of day-to-day life will be.[14]

HUMAN EXCELLENCE

The standards that I have discussed are not agreed upon simply or altogether. On the contrary: they are controversial matters among various thinkers. The various ways of life and philosophical views of politics are guided by different but related understandings of human excellence. Discussing these differences will help us better to understand these ways and the nature of the basic political phenomena. I will describe and discuss each view, show how they can open to other views, and indicate their common sense or natural origin.

Plato's *Republic* is the classic presentation. The philosopher is the ruler of the best regime, whose purpose is to educate philosophers. It is just to give to each that for which its nature suits it. That is, to be just is to distribute goods and tasks equally and unequally because our natures are unequal. What is best for the philosopher and the political rulers from whom the philosophers emerge is not a superfluity of goods or even private property, and not tyrannical pleasure or even a private family. It is, therefore, not a situation that most would choose. The philosophers seek what truly is, not what is fleeting, seek to understand the "ideas" in relation to what is good, and are also trained mathematically. Their knowledge is directed to what is higher than ordinary knowledge but, nonetheless, related to or on a line with it because the opinions and trust that usually guide us reflect what truly is.[15] The philosophical life is a search, with knowledge obtained but limited. It is a fuller and freer use of our speech or reason than are other lives because it seeks a comprehensive articulation of significant matters such as virtue, love, beauty, and the best regime, as well as of general issues such as sameness, otherness, rest, motion, and being. As a search it is also passionate, although devoted to calm undisturbed examination, with the pleasure connected to this. It does not piously bow down to gods, to the mysteriously unknowable, to reigning opinion, or rest on presumed knowledge that is unexamined. In this sense, philosophy is spirited and courageous, properly fearing ignorance but not frozen in its face.

Such a philosophical life is discovered and encouraged as the best life and is a new life, historically. Even the most just political community is limited in its excellence because it deals with ordinary goods such as honor and wealth and with individuals who cannot devote themselves completely to what is common. Indeed, although both philosophers and the rest of us seek to possess what we believe to be good, the discrepancy between the goods that they and we seek concretely is too great to allow philosophers actually to rule. The best regime is impossible in the flesh.

Indicating this limit is one of Plato's purposes in the *Republic*. But the philosopher himself is possible and can come to be and even for a while be preserved in an aristocracy, or in a democracy if it has sufficient individual virtue and an aristocratic or leisured group within it.

Plato's philosopher is a compelling and radical picture of human excellence. The *Republic* also describes other regimes, however, chief among them a regime devoted to training those dominated by spiritedness so that they are governed by ethical virtue. It is from these "guardians" that rulers and then philosophers emerge. Socrates also describes a regime governed by spiritedness but dedicated to honor rather than to virtue that is first in line after the fall of the philosophers' regime.

The Platonic ruler governed by ethical virtue is devoted to the community and does not engage in tyrannical excess. One might compare such a ruler to Aristotle's example of complete ethical virtue, his man of great pride. Aristotle's great-souled man, however, also enjoys political prudence, judgment, or practical wisdom to a degree that Plato does not always make explicit but that his Socrates often displays. So we may say that after the philosopher the next type celebrated is the statesman, who has a range of soul that permits all the virtues, political wisdom, and devotion to the common good. We may think of Washington, Lincoln, and Churchill as exemplifying this life, if we adjust for the political parties, equality in rights, and technology of modern democracy. An exalted version of the ordinary—Aristotelian statesmanship—and the radical attempt to discover an extraordinary true world—Platonic philosophy—are always attractive models of human excellence.

A link between philosophical and political excellence is the founding of regimes: the legislator or founder is another instance of human greatness who, indeed, is often portrayed as godlike. Founding goes beyond prudently securing the justice of one's country or its defense. For it involves choosing what is just generally in practices and institutions and not only in particular measures. Such choice requires both general and particular knowledge and is developed especially in Plato's *Laws* and Aristotle's *Politics*, and exemplified in our own founding.

Is such founding or legislating chiefly political or philosophical? It is primarily philosophical because the translation of a principled understanding of what is good (happiness), just, and properly individual to a view of what could be best politically is philosophical. Still, actually transforming this understanding into a regime that organizes people and territory now and in the future is political.[16]

The next great radical notion of human perfection is the one who walks righteously on a divine path—the saint, we might say, and those who are more ordinarily pious. We see, particularly in Christianity, a possible generalizing of the philosophical but, especially, a de-intellectualizing of the purity that is connected to or inspired by the objects of the philosophical life and the philosophical life itself.[17] This saintly purity may attempt to disregard nature, but it cannot overcome natural limits of time, space, and hunger, although it can ignore (or claim to ignore) the usual physical pleasures and political interests. Saintliness, prophesy, closeness to god or the gods carries or tries to carry with it its own unchallenged or, indeed, unchallengeable validity. Nonetheless, we can discuss and evaluate it in human terms when we consider its characteristics in the light of human powers and its regime in the light of human justice and compare it to the alternatives.

Saintliness shares with philosophy and other novel claims of human excellence the radicalism that often attracts. The saint and a demand for saintliness, observance, or belief also lead to a particular view of rule, namely, priestly rule or denigration of the political and economic. Not the statesman or the philosopher but the worldly representative of the holy rules. The Machiavellian revolution against this puts forward as the emblematic human being the prince. In doing so it upends the traditional notion of virtue and the notion of the "altogether good" behavior of a saintly or observant kind. The prince is a founder of what seems novel: he is enterprising but also managerial, and shapes his new people. He creates the standards that govern others, and in terms of which he is exemplary. The elements that resemble Aristotle in Machiavelli differ from him because Machiavellian virtuous activity is not measured or tied to specific passions and goods, political honor becomes glory given by a people that you have yourself formed, the exalted life is in fact a princely creation, philosophy or science comes to serve interests other than knowledge itself, and the miracles of saints are treated as the mechanisms of princes.

The interrelations among the exemplary ways of life show perhaps more directly than conceptual discussions the nature of the historical links of understanding and reaction from which different judgments emerge. Prophesy may predate Christianity and theoretical reflection,

but its interpretation in the revealed religions is influenced philosophically. Machiavelli's discussion reacts to the dominance of religious rule. The historical interrelations continue, as we will see. They
affect how human possibilities and their associated pleasures come
to light and, especially, how they are brought together and discussed.
Seemingly novel views of human excellence take natural possibilities
of virtue, purity, the elements of the soul, the common good, and
other matters and highlight and develop them in certain ways. But
they do not create these possibilities, or change their natural rank.

The next great example of human excellence is the securer of individual rights: the more democratic or widespread version of Machiavelli's prince is our entrepreneur or captain of industry together with
the increasingly secure, tame, and practically nice or "good" people.
Acquisition and conquering nature become the central tasks, and the
"rational and industrious few" dominated by responsibility and other
modern virtues and, increasingly, by enlightenment become the model
figures. The working out of various elements of this figure characterizes much Anglo-American thought from Hobbes and Locke on. The
entrepreneur and, especially, the great scientific discoverer becomes
at once radical and useful. The ends served remain natural: the point
is to satisfy desire, reduce poverty, and increase health and safety. Ordinary natural limits to satisfaction are loosened but still in order to
serve natural ends.

The next model figure is Rousseau's romantic. Just as the other
radical figures are considered to be most fully free, so, too, with Rousseau's romantic, who develops existent possibilities of the unity or
balance of desire and its satisfaction but in what might now appear to
be (but is not) a new, not always possible, human being: the nonaspi-
rational satisfier of eros. Such a figure is a version of the love that
gazes only at the initially exquisite but, in fact, incomplete. In a more
ordinary sense this becomes the quasi-mystical romanticism of the
couple that is "meant to be." It is also a beginning of the notion of
the unique and ineffable artistic "genius" as the exemplary being. But
one wonders whether such a genius is not in fact a compound of previously understood artistic excellence and purity. This is not to say
that no new developments of the possibilities of art and music come
into being, but it is to say that the "genius" does not differ in whatever

true excellence he has from the artistic excellence of the past or that the high rank of some art was previously ignored.[18]

The romantic can never be fully at home politically. But Rousseau also finds or develops a more ordinary excellence, namely, devoted citizenship based on will. The general "will" that Rousseau considers leads to the next picture of freedom, not philosophical yet universal in its enlightened rationality: the liberal individual now connected to equal morality, the only full and equal self-legislation. Reason casts the arc under which nature and human action have meaning, causally and morally. Morality is not temporal but is outside of time. Yet temporal history brings us as close as we might come to realizing factually the demands of this morality, such as perpetual peace. This Kantian notion, too, however, is intelligible in terms of and challenged by natural understanding, as I argued in my discussions of virtue.

The moral being as hero does not differentiate the ordinary from the excellent. He is supplanted or supplemented by Hegel's final hero: the man who unifies himself as a universal citizen in a complex state. He combines Rousseau's unity and balance, Kant's moral excellence, Locke's reasonable industry, rational faith, and full understanding. He is completely unalienated, the exemplary citizen of the *Rechtsstaat*, the just state, at the end of history, free because living under a rationality that overcomes all contradiction, not only generally, but in and for himself. He is the chief citizen whose work is most completely dedicated to the community, who exemplifies ethical virtue not as prudent statesmanship but as the rational or legal judgment of a senior bureaucrat, indeed, a wise philosophy professor who under his rational umbrella also brings out the meaning of art and religion. Such a figure's virtue is not radically different from the ordinary excellence of the citizen of such a state, but he is more directly self-conscious. Fantastic as such complete knowledge might seem, it follows philosophy's natural goal from its beginning—wisdom—and Hegel's claims can in the end be judged in natural terms.[19]

In principle this is Marx's man as well: free, equal, and unalienated but with no exceptional bureaucrats or philosophy professors who are more completely dedicated than are others to what is universal. The next great exemplary figure, the next great discovery or imposition of such a being, is Nietzsche's, where not will to morality or reason but to power, to creative organizing, is central: the super-man. The superman is once again a radical and alluring figure, not an equal man. He is a creative figure beyond merely cognitive, moral, and ethical shaping; he is one who also rationalizes or makes meaning-ful the irrational, the drives, fully shaping what history has brought, following his own sense of good (value) and of the common (jus-tice). In Nietzsche, nothing is exemplary in the ordinary, but one does find in his thought a modern unity of the political and the philo-sophical. As with others, the novelty in Nietzsche arises from fo-cusing on and developing natural possibilities of rule, command, reverence, and truth that are already visible in the classics. Histori-cally, in fact, loyalty to self and self-overcoming are already developed in Rousseau and Hegel, as well as being present naturally. So, too, is the significance of art. Indeed, the view of thinkers and statesmen as creators is visible in Machiavelli—and art as "knowledge" is already evident in the *Republic*.

In Heidegger, finally, the exemplary figure strikes the reader as the authentic man, much as Heidegger denies that he intends this. Au-thenticity attempts to bring to the fore and in that sense to place us within the radical openness of our being. It permits an equality, as one's own, within a people, although we are led by the understanding of philosophers, poets, and statesmen. I have discussed throughout the book whether we can successfully understand in other ways the substance of what Heidegger brings forward in his view of human being and what is meaningful.

Conclusion

My examinations of the nature of fundamental political phenomena do not require an overall conclusion. Still, it will be useful to indicate again my basic standpoint and the links among my discussions. The ambiguity of such a summary can be clarified by returning to the original discussions from which it is drawn.

Practical activity begins within contexts that provide meaning to actions and things. These contexts depend on the broadest practical context, the regime or way of life. Ways of life are formed by the goods or purposes to which they are directed and the common order, the view of justice, that governs how we distribute tasks, things, and opportunities. What makes particular goods or ends worthwhile is a general understanding of the goodness, the choiceworthiness, of things and actions. We always implicitly project in advance and are immersed within a way of life and the understanding of what is good and just that comprise its direction and intelligibility, its meaning. This meaning is the heart of the trust in and expectations that we have of others, the character and virtue that forms us, and the place of punishment and law.

Our activities and experiences, including our experiences of the passions, are formed primarily by speech and reason, in forms such as calculation, judgment, deliberation, recognition, prudence, and opinion. These possibilities of discussion, the presence of pleasure, the exigencies of war, and the possibility of founding or instituting regimes enable us in some circumstances to question elements of our way of life—freedom, property, virtue, and so on—and perhaps the way of life itself. This questioning is more difficult the more completely a way of life identifies just or righteous procedures and actions with what is good. Nonetheless, no regime can be completely closed, and this openness, this cosmopolitanism, together with a way of life's reliance on and projection of an "ontological" horizon still more complex than what is significant politically, affords us the possibility of questioning.

When we consider basic political phenomena we first implicitly have in mind the regime from which they draw their meaning and from which we draw our examples. This dependence is obscured by the theoretical results of science, philosophy, and political philosophy, so that we today have traditions and professions that deal with academic puzzles, and notions that often obscure or take for granted elements of the phenomena and the existence of theoretical study itself. Bringing this issue to the surface was a central task of thinkers such as Husserl and Heidegger and their students, and remains an ongoing concern.

Although the dependence of political phenomena on their regimes must not be forgotten, it is mitigated by the ways we can examine these phenomena separately and can compare ways of life generally. This examination points ultimately to the fullest presence of a phenomenon within the most complete way of life.

After discussing the nature of practical action I turned to the phenomenon of freedom. To be free is to be self-directed and unchained, and this suggests a readiness, openness, and steadiness in relation to goods and activities that are intelligible and desirable in certain ways, that is, as we see them in terms of a certain meaning. Ultimately, the most complete freedom is connected to the most complete meaning of actions and things, the fullest excellence and intelligibility.

Freedom also belongs to an implicit and, then, philosophically explicit understanding of the soul or self about whom we have expectations for just or righteous actions, and to whom what is good is distributed. Central in this understanding is a view of the basic movements of the soul, which first come to light in Plato's discussion of eros and thumos. I describe in my chapter on freedom and rights the orientation of these movements, and their connection to reason.

The understanding of rights involves elements that we interpret differently in different ways of life, something that is also true of what can be good or just. These views are not merely irreconcilable or relative, however. What is general in them largely receives its meaning from what is possible and can occur in the fullest way of life, so that we can see or attempt to see the others as declines or declensions from this. This attempt cannot be completely successful, however, because the understanding of our spirited independence and the inviolability and self-reverence we see in our defense of equal rights is not simply compatible with the classical orientation to what is noble or excellent and, therefore, unequal in our pride, reason, love, and friendships. Rights stem from the protection and inviolability of one's own, one's own individuality, which, politically, we cannot make fully compatible with what is best simply. Still, both liberal democracy and classical regimes are linked by these basic powers of our soul and by their orientation to an understanding of what is just and good.

We cannot elaborate the differences and ranks among ways of life without discussing the phenomenon of political power, and our human powers and virtues. Our distinctive abilities are our reason, reason's forming of our passions, and the experiences of pleasure connected to this. Human excellence is the full or beautiful use of these powers—their full and fitting use. The full use is their virtuous use, employing our powers in relation to goods and passions in a manner that is neither excessive nor insufficient. Our powers indicate their proper use through pleasure, pain, and measured judgment. This indication, however, is not sufficient to guarantee such use. In any event, something's power cannot be stripped from it, or amalgamated with other powers, or truncated in its use without the thing itself being distorted.

Liberal democracy's approach to power is one of the phenomena that indicates its comprehensiveness as a regime, with its understanding of the self and what is good primarily in terms of security and relieving unease; of power and pleasure as something to be added up and amalgamated but not essentially tied to and differentiated in terms of varied activities; and with its view of virtue as connected to securing us in our rights rather than using our abilities nobly or beautifully. To use our abilities beautifully is to use them in a way that fits their object, that enables us to stand out attractively, and that fosters the presence of distinctive pleasures composed from the full range of pleasure's possibilities—purity, intensity, completion, and so on. Taken together, virtues comprise a character that allows both success or happiness—the enjoyment of goods understood in a certain way—and the trustworthiness or reliability on which just distribution in common enterprises depends.

Liberal democratic regimes, therefore, have distinctive virtues such as responsibility and toleration that are connected to the regime's other features. But they also rely on egalitarian versions of classical virtues and, privately if not publicly, on the fuller understanding of pleasure, what is good, and proper distribution that we see in the classical aspiration to statesmanship and aristocracy. This duality is true as well of property. Property is justified both by best use and by what I need for my independence and separateness. These justifications are the heart of the substance of justice, which is a form of equal to equals and unequal to unequals. Once developed, these justifications of property point to different directions or emphases in classical and liberal regimes—the expansion of available goods in liberal democracies, and putting them in the best hands, classically.

It is especially in liberal democratic regimes that we can address still other phenomena of political life such as legitimacy, representation, and separation of powers, because it is in such regimes that these phenomena come to light and are coherent with the meaning of the regime as a whole. The three fundamental ways of life I emphasized are classical and liberal democratic regimes and religious ways. I argued that we can basically find the meaning of classical democracy in the understanding of nobility, the variety of pleasure, and the differentiation of citizenship and expectations that we find in classical aristocracy. Still, classical democracy's emphasis on freedom links it to post-Machiavellian modernity. The classical and the modern differ, but they are also connected and overlap: we cannot altogether separate the modern meaning of power, virtue, and property from the more complete natural and classical meaning on which they rely and to which they point. I also indicated what I judge to be the limits of religious regimes, although not of faith itself.

The meaning that forms regimes points to a still wider horizon, one that we project and see because we need to experience and describe what is good, what is just, and the soul in terms of motion, completion, what makes something common or whole, and what allows it to be separate or independent. An understanding of satisfaction and completion, of movement and motivation, of what is common, independent, and separate, of meaningful space and time and similar matters: all this is involved implicitly and at times explicitly in the contexts and ways of life to which we belong. They are not after the fact generalizations but the components from which the fundamental political concepts take or spell out their meaning in the matters with which political and human life deal. One reason the philosophical life is the most beautiful or comprehensive use of our powers is because it deals with the most comprehensive phenomena. The intellectual difficulty in understanding how things can be precisely what they are but also belong to what is common or whole, and independent yet also unified, is reflected in the political and ethical problem of the relation between what is one's own and what is good and the other issues I discussed.

I also intended the discussion of this wider horizon to take into account Heidegger's notion of man and being but without ascribing modes of being to phantasms or the objects of academic specialties or sciences, and without considering our human end or enclosure to be only a people and our own outward extension toward the possibility of dying. For our end and identity also involve what is cosmopolitan in that to which we aspire and in that which we defend.

I also attempted to take into account the possibility of novelty and of the difference between human things and what we can see through modern physical science. An objection to my standpoint, which tries to understand practical and theoretical activity by linking what we project in advance and take for granted with the nature of things seen primarily in classical terms, is that it fails to account for what is fundamentally novel and historical. In various ways I attempted to develop the grounds from within what is lasting of how we can develop what is apparently or practically (but perforce not fundamentally) novel. I also examined various questions raised by historicism, culture, technology, and materialism in order to indicate the continuing salience of the natural standpoint.

The importance of variety in ways of life might appear to denigrate the significance of the bodily and concrete. In addition to my discussions of change and what is historical, I attempted to clarify the salience of what is bodily and particular by examining patriotism and other interpretations of the connection between particular and general in politics, the status of the body in relation to the soul, questions of identity, and the status of what appears to be identical or universal in all ways of life (and not only what is cosmopolitan in them in the sense that they reflect different views and experiences of freedom, justice, virtue, power, property, and what is good). Our ordinary beginnings, the usual necessities and distinctions with which we deal, help set the direction for the fullest use of our powers. These beginnings are treated differently in different regimes and can to a remarkable extent be changed. But the effect on our aspirations and understanding of attempting to overcome our first limits and beginnings may not always be salutary.

I closed my analysis by discussing various notions of human excellence. One might ask whether anything today or in the future could add to, reform, or replace these notions. Perhaps here, however, as with judging the merit of possible changes in human characteristics themselves, modesty is in order. We can continue to address and discover what is novel by developing aspects of things that we have left in the shadows. But it is best if this would be done based on permanent standards of excellence. In the last analysis we do not require something new but, rather, attention to the permanent basis of justice, freedom, and beauty, to the powers of the soul, and to political excellence and the philosophical life. Perhaps what is radical today is not the exciting but the responsible, not the novel but the natural, not the immediate but the rational, and not the arbitrary but the free.

NOTES

Introduction

1. Although my study concerns political phenomena and does not directly interpret texts, many of the remarkable recent studies of Plato, Aristotle, Machiavelli, Locke, Kant, Hegel, Nietzsche, Heidegger, and others help us to understand political phenomena more immediately.

2. In thinking about how characteristics can be common, one should consider the varieties of commonality. Some common characteristics can be uniform among their members as, say, each instance of the number 2 is identical, but some can differ among them as, say, the degree of reason differs among us, or as I and my shadow are alike but differ. I discuss in later chapters the varieties of commonality.

3. I will use "politics" and "political life" equivalently.

4. Reason and speech differ. Speech can involve exclamations, assertions, deceptions, promises, incantations—rhetoric. Nonetheless, all speech is in the end oriented to speaking truly because the distinctions, connections, and goals that constitute its intelligibility rest on natural distinctions, connections, and goals. Although I will only occasionally make speech my theme, my discussions of history and nature, the particular and the general, freedom and what is common, and other subjects will in effect also consider the relation between speaking and reason, whose goal is to speak truly. We can translate the Greek *logos* as either speech or reason, which shows their basic connection, a connection more revealing than a strict distinction between, say, talking and reasoning or speaking as external and reasoning as internal would be.

5. Consider here the notion that in time "sedimentation" covers over the basic experiences from which concepts emerge. See, e.g., Edmund Husserl, *The Crisis of the European Sciences*, trans. David Carr (Evanston, IL: Northwestern University Press, 1970), first published in German in 1936; and Leo Strauss's notion of the second cave or the cave beneath the cave, e.g., in Leo Strauss, *Persecution and the Art of Writing* (Glencoe, IL: Free Press, 1952), 152–57; and Leo Strauss, *Philosophy and Revelation*, trans. Eve Adler (Albany: SUNY Press, 1995), first published in German in 1935.

6. I mean "modern" in the sense of after Machiavelli and Descartes. For Descartes, see Martin Heidegger, *Being and Time*, trans. John Macquarrie and Edward Robinson (New York: Harper and Row, 1962), first published in German in 1927; and Martin Heidegger, *Nietzsche*, trans. David Farrell Krell (New York: Harper and Row, 1977), first published in German in 1961; and Richard Kennington, *On Modern Origins*, ed. Pamela Kraus and Frank Hunt (Lanham, MD: Lexington Books, 2004), chs. 6–11.

7. In any event, this similarity or identity seems clear to us, in our way of life.

8. One can compare not only the elements of regimes but also political wholes themselves in terms of justice. In both cases this comparison allows concepts to be uncovered. The central political phenomena are speech or opinion laden and are thus open to becoming conceptually understood.

9. Nietzsche's *Beyond Good and Evil* provides a good illustration of the variability among thinkers in what counts as a problem. See Friedrich Nietzsche, *Beyond Good and Evil*, trans. Walter Kaufmann (New York: Vintage Books, 1966), pt. 1, sec. 1; first published in German in 1886. See also Michael Polanyi, *The Tacit Dimension* (Garden City, NY: Doubleday & Company, 1966).

10. See Heidegger, *Being and Time*; Plato, *Republic*, trans. Allan Bloom (New York: Basic Books, 1968, 1991); G. W. F. Hegel, *Elements of the Philosophy of Right*, ed. Allen W. Wood, trans. H. W. Nisbet (Cambridge: Cambridge University Press, 1991), first published in German in 1821; and Thomas Hobbes, *Leviathan*, ed. Richard Tuck (Cambridge: Cambridge University Press, 1991), first published in 1651.

11. One way theoretical discussion shows its connection to ordinary affairs is through thinkers' manner of presentation or writing, where they must consider the effect of their teachings on their community, their supporters and friends within their communities, their students within their communities, and their future students, friends, and foes. See Strauss, *Persecution and the Art of Writing*.

12. In Heidegger's discussion, understanding, meaning, and questionability arise from and ultimately return to the "world" in which we are im-

mersed and from our human mode of being (the "existentials"). Each of our actions, and the concepts that emerge from them, belongs together in the (historically variable) worlds in which we are immersed. See Martin Heidegger, *History of the Concept of Time*, trans. Theodore Kisiel (Bloomington: Indiana University Press, 1985), first published in German in 1979, from lectures delivered in 1925; Heidegger, *Being and Time*; Edmund Husserl, *Logical Investigations*, trans. J. H. Findlay (New York: Routledge, 1970), first published in German in 1901–2; Nietzsche, *Beyond Good and Evil*; and various writings of Wilhelm Dilthey, e.g., *Introduction to the Human Sciences*, ed. Rudolf A. Makkreel and Frithjof Rodl (Princeton, NJ: Princeton University Press, 1989), first published in German 1883.

13. For Klein, consider Jacob Klein, *Greek Mathematical Thought and the Origin of Algebra*, trans. Eva Brann (Cambridge, MA: MIT Press, 1968), first published in German in 1934, 1936.

14. It is also to recognize how theoretically formed, how sedimented, our contemporary world is.

15. Others argue that we must begin from a necessary, if hidden, stage of historical development, or from our most powerful drives. I will discuss these views in due course.

16. See Heidegger, *Being and Time*; and Martin Heidegger, *Zollikon Seminars*, ed. Medard Boss, trans. Franz Mayr and Richard Askay (Evanston, IL: Northwestern University Press, 2001), first published in German in 1987.

17. Consider how Plato begins many of his dialogues, Aristotle's ethical and political works and their emphasis on *pragmata* (things), and Heidegger's discussions of Aristotle.

18. One should be wary of Heidegger practically because of his support of the Nazis and theoretically because of what in his views allowed this to happen. We should be cautious about the classics because of their preceding modern science, their not recognizing equal natural rights, and the existence of slavery in ancient cities. Wariness and caution, however, are warnings, not arguments.

19. I will sometimes use the term "regime" to designate the broadest context of political activity, and sometimes way of life. I will use these terms interchangeably. "Way of life" is the more fundamental term because it includes things, actions, and qualities that today we tend to believe are not or should not be political. But the contemporary restrictions that allow independence or privacy in economic and religious life result from the political choice that established liberal democracy. Ways of life are essentially political because actions are always subject to authoritative constitutional or legal choice that fits them together into a whole. Indeed, the dominant opinion about justice in a way of life governs who pursues which activities and

who can use and enjoy which goods. This opinion is announced or mandated in law and culture, or in divine writings and priestly control. A view of what goods it is proper to pursue and, indeed, what is good or choiceworthy about them, their goodness, is also fundamental, for it sets the purposes of communities and their citizens. So the term "way of life" captures this breadth of justice and goods, while the term "regime"—democracy, liberal democracy, oligarchy, aristocracy, tyranny—captures what is politically authoritative. I intend my discussion of context and concepts to show their basis in ways of life that are politically ordered but also to indicate what is inevitably cosmopolitan in our actions.

I also will mention the country or the "city," in the sense of the classical polis, as the unit formed by a regime, or following a way of life. The country—"America"—evokes our way of life rather than our mere territory or state but also evokes *our* way of life rather than a similar regime elsewhere. But I do not mean this indication to close discussion. The questions of patriotism, loyalty, identity, and the relation between general and particular will be among those I will address.

20. The place of theoretical issues is also important in some of the variants of liberal democracy (such as Hegel's German *Rechtsstatt*) that follow. See John Locke, *Essay Concerning Human Understanding*, ed. Peter Nidditch (Oxford: Oxford University Press, 1975), first published in 1689; and John Locke, *Two Treatises of Government*, ed. Peter Laslett (Cambridge: Cambridge University Press, 1960), first published in 1690. For Locke generally, consider, among others, Peter Myers, *Our Only Star and Compass* (Lanham, MD: Rowman and Littlefield, 1999); Thomas Pangle, *The Spirit of Modern Republicanism* (Chicago: University of Chicago Press), 1987; and Michael Zuckert, *Launching Liberalism* (Lawrence: University Press of Kansas, 2002).

CHAPTER ONE.   The Nature of Practical Action

1. I will concentrate on "context" because, although to speak of contexts, let alone to analyze what a context is, is already post-philosophical—would one discuss "contexts" in a world dominated by myths and gods?—it is both a recognizable and largely neutral term for us.

2. Nonetheless, as I indicated, different coughs in different situations call forth different reactions—stifling or treatment, say, that, together with the origin, belongs to how the cough is experienced and heard. There is no simple subject "cough" experienced with different predicates. The cough is always this or that type of cough, including a "mere" cough: it is always a

meaningful cough. The "mere" cough can then be seen to have qualities common across almost all coughs—most obviously its (unstifled) sound. (The distinction between subject and predicates is for many matters an analytical more than an experienced one.)

3. The gun or potential gun may be experienced as threatening or not, a display object or not, military, or private. It is still seen and to a large degree experienced as a "gun," which means that it looks and acts a certain way and that one can and always is implicitly locating it in a context of harm, danger, and defense. (If one has never seen a gun one is mystified about it, i.e., does not understand its context and its function within this. Once it is used its effect is common enough that its function becomes clear.) What counts as experienced danger and appropriate response, however, differs with different ways of life and their individual virtues. This connection to different regimes limits the degree to which guns or arms will be separated from other factors and developed on their own to their fullest destructive capacity. So one might say that the gun is experienced commonly in relation to shape and power, that this function and what is connected to it (fear, defense, security) is universal to a degree, but that both one's reaction to the gun and how far one will go in isolating and developing it depend on the reigning notions of property, expectations, and defense, which are not identical everywhere. Is one in a warrior country, is one training, are weapons public, etc.? Plato's *Statesman* gives a good example of thinking through various modes of protection and defense. Plato, *Statesman*, trans. Seth Benardete (Chicago: University of Chicago Press, 1986), 279c8-280a4.

4. This is one reason that lying can obscure what is actually happening.

5. As I have said, the most universal things and characteristics are not always what is fullest and most meaningful. One characteristic that appears to be universal among humans that does belong to or constitute something vital is attachment to one's own, to one's own individuality and possible improvement, even if it is to oneself as contributing to common tasks. Even this individuality, however, is interpreted and developed in different ways, as we will see in my discussions of freedom and rights.

Differences of context are not especially significant for, say, noticing animals, but they are significant for using them and for producing things. Central in clarifying this issue is the degree of independence that belongs to the members of a class and the independence, basic uses, and special uses of non-human things. Various members of animal species look alike and are self-generating and are so noticed but are used or not according to political regime, culture, and necessity. This use can bring out their powers more fully than can their common look and actions. We can, for example, point them out in terms of special qualities for use and training (police dogs, circus animals), consumption, worship (sacred cows), or as individual objects of affection, where we give them names. Some of these qualities seem connected to the animal itself and others almost completely imposed on it—the cow's sacredness, say. The degree to which universal or average characteristics remain basic in any developed excellence and use is a significant question that I will address in what follows. What is cosmopolitan across ways of life, moreover, is not only or primarily what is average but also possibilities, aspirations, and excellences that are always present yet in different degrees, and rarely reached or, sometimes, even noticed.

6. See Mark Blitz, *Conserving Liberty* (Stanford, CA: Hoover Institution Press, 2011), ch. 4.

7. The meaningful as what is important and what guides can affect not just me, but my community or beyond. In each case, meaning implicitly or explicitly raises the question of true guidance, significance, intelligibility, and direction, the range of purpose and degree of direction.

The notion of meaning as intention—I meant to do that, I mean to make this argument, I mean to take this trip—is a version of meaning as guidance and intelligibility: an intention produces or brings out the intelligibility of the actions and steps one takes or words one says, guided by one's end or goal. Meaning in the sense of implication or suggestion—"this, however, does not mean . . . "—is also connected to intelligibility, to meaning as linking or orienting, as belonging to an order.

8. I am using common sense and practical judgment equivalently here. If they are used differently, practical judgment emphasizes understanding particulars within a context and, even, affecting it, and common sense emphasizes operating within it.

9. For a discussion of intuition and analytic philosophy, see Stanley Rosen, *The Limits of Analysis* (New York: Basic Books, 1980), 3–27.

10. When we say that someone has common sense we are referring largely to the actions of ordinary life.

11. This can to a degree (and not always usefully) be replaced or enforced by law when necessary. Sharp dealers are those who push to the limits of ordinary acceptability. For trust, consider, among others, Francis Fukuyama, *Trust* (New York: Free Press, 1995); Russell Hardin, *Trust and Trustworthiness* (New York: Russell Sage Foundation, 2004); Masamichi Sasaki, ed., *Trust in Contemporary Society* (Leiden: Brill, 2019); and Kevin Vallier, *Must Politics Be War?* (Oxford: Oxford University Press, 2019). See, too, Jacob Howland, *Glaucon's Fate* (Philadelphia: Paul Dry Books, 2018), 194.

12. The link between opinion and reputation, what we and others say about what is appropriate and expected and how confidently we trust others, is the Greek *doxa*, translated as "opinion" and originating in seeing (appear-

ing) and reputation. See Plato's *Republic* and other dialogues that discuss virtues, such as the *Laches*, *Theages*, and *Charmides*. Plato, *Laches*, trans. James H. Nichols Jr., in *The Roots of Political Philosophy: Ten Forgotten Socratic Dialogues*, ed. Thomas L. Pangle (Ithaca, NY: Cornell University Press, 1987); Plato, *Theages*, trans. Thomas L. Pangle, in Pangle, *The Roots of Political Philosophy*; Plato, *Charmides*, trans. Thomas G. West and Grace Starry West (Indianapolis IN: Hackett, 1986).

For Plato generally, consider, among other works, Eva Brann, *The Music of the Republic* (Philadelphia: Paul Dry Books, 2004); Mark Blitz and J. Michael Hoffpauir, eds., *Plato's Political Thought* (New York: Oxford Bibliographies, 2019); Mark Blitz, *Plato's Political Philosophy* (Baltimore, MD: Johns Hopkins University Press, 2010); Christopher Bruell, *On the Socratic Education* (Lanham, MD: Rowman and Littlefield, 1999); Leon Harold Craig, *The War Lover* (Toronto: University of Toronto Press, 1996); Jacob Howland, *Glaucon's Fate* (Philadelphia: Paul Dry Books, 2018); Stanley Rosen, *Plato's Republic* (New Haven, CT: Yale University Press, 2005); Stanley Rosen, *Plato's Sophist* (New Haven, CT: Yale University Press, 1983); Devin Stauffer, *Plato's Introduction to the Question of Justice* (Albany: SUNY Press, 2000); Leo Strauss, *The City and Man* (New York: Rand McNally, 1963); and Catherine H. Zuckert, *Plato's Philosophers* (Chicago: University of Chicago Press, 2009).

13. How far this reliable expectation must go—whether it reaches to a shared understanding of gods and the cosmos, say—is another question, as are the issues of how explicit this understanding of our way must be. Similarly open for now is the question of true virtue, character, trust, and reputation. My point here is that implicit expectations are involved in the various connected actions of a people or place and that the usual horizon for these expectations is the political order.

14. In John Locke's understanding, which is fundamental for liberal democracy, satisfying desire and experiencing pleasure are seen as relieving unease rather than as substantive enjoyment. The result is to split satisfaction and pleasure as much as possible from specific activities. See Locke, *An Essay Concerning Human Understanding*, bk. II, ch. 21. See also Hobbes, *Leviathan*, ch. 6.

15. In terms of what I have said about nature, what we do not make in practical affairs and what is always there in any practical effort is that they are embedded in a pre-view of goodness and of a common order of expected actions, opportunities, procedures, and distributions.

16. Philosophically, we then also see Hegel's and Nietzsche's attempted improvement to or overturning of bourgeois life: the goodness of things as allowing continued movement to what is Absolutely free or as permitting

creative mastery. For Hegel generally, consider, among other works, Paul Franco, *Hegel's Philosophy of Freedom* (New Haven, CT: Yale University Press, 1999); Dean Moyer, ed., *The Oxford Handbook of Hegel* (New York: Oxford University Press, 2017); and Steven Smith, *Hegel's Critique of Liberalism* (Chicago: University of Chicago Press, 1989). For Nietzsche, consider, among others, Peter Berkowitz, *Nietzsche: The Ethics of an Immoralist* (Cambridge, MA: Harvard University Press, 1995); Michael Allen Gillespie, *Nietzsche's Final Teaching* (Chicago: University of Chicago Press, 2017); Lawrence Lampert, *What a Philosopher Is: Becoming Nietzsche* (Chicago: University of Chicago Press, 2017); and Heinrich Meier, *Nietzsches Vermachtnis* (Munich: C. H. Beck, 2019).

17. I will discuss justice and what is good more fully in what follows.

18. When I examined the contexts of our activities we saw that they relied on and implicitly pushed forward to (and in a sense began from) life within our (liberal democratic) regime and the view of justice and what can be good that constitute the regime and how one can choose within it. "Culture" (and specific contexts) shows the regime and its elements at work, embodied, alive: what, say, "liberty" means today and how it is at work in this particular activity today. So the same smart young men who a generation ago became physicians now have daughters who become physicians and sons who work in technology and finance. Nonetheless, variations in contemporary mores remain less essential for first guiding our actions than are our regime's general opinions and expectations.

19. This opposes a classical view in which we have practical choices in the light of the unchanging although unreachable. For Heidegger, too, as for Nietzsche, but on a different level, everything is supremely separate—epochs of being, human possibilities, theory and practice—but also completely connected, within epochs of being or in being itself.

20. This is a chief problem of our culture. We are intellectually and politically better advised to bring to the surface the phenomena of justice, thought, and art that the general term "culture" hides, and thereby increase our ability to uncover natural standards. This possibility always exists and is the implicit source of the revivals within our own culture of more natural music and narrative.

21. One might consider Tocqueville's *Democracy in America* in this light, too: democracy is the social condition that shapes everything in democratic America; the democratic way of life as it develops in turn affects the understanding of democracy itself.

22. I do this as well to indicate various natural bases of change and, therefore, to deal with historicist views that suggest that significant change is in the last analysis a matter of fate.

23. Forbidden flesh is (naturally) attractive, which is why it sometimes needs to be forbidden. Consider the status of "epicureanism" as a danger to religion.

24. Consider Plato's *Statesman*.

25. Consider Plato's *Laws. The Laws of Plato*, trans. Thomas L. Pangle (Chicago: University of Chicago Press, 1988).

26. See Plato's *Laches*.

27. This element of opinion and of separation is missing in Heidegger's discussion of the public and people in *Being and Time*. He writes there that "everything good is a heritage" (435).

28. Heidegger argues that grasping afresh the basic mode of being that underlies a science or scholarly discipline is central to significant new developments in it. Loosening or addressing the view of space, time, history, or the holy is the key to deeper understanding of the matter with which these sciences deal. This understanding, moreover, need not, indeed, usually is not, found directly within the sciences themselves but in better grasping the everyday range and meaning of the phenomena and mode of being on which the science in question depends. Theology and art criticism, indeed, are apt to block rather than to grant access to the phenomena from which they originally spring.

29. Consider Susan Meld Shell, ed., *The Strauss-Krüger Correspondence: Returning to Plato through Kant* (London: Palgrave Macmillan, 2018).

30. Consider, e.g., Rousseau's discussion in his *Discourse on the Origin of Inequality*, first published in 1755. Jean-Jacques Rousseau, *The Discourses and Other Political Writings*, ed. Victor Gourevitch (Cambridge: Cambridge University Press, 1997). For Rousseau generally, consider, among others, Arthur Melzer, *The Natural Goodness of Man* (Chicago: University of Chicago Press, 1990); and Leo Strauss, *Natural Right and History* (Chicago: University of Chicago Press, 1953).

31. See Karl Lowith, *Meaning in History* (Chicago: University of Chicago Press, 1949).

32. The serious historicisms are not contradictory or simple—by "simple," I mean have no grasp of why their own concepts, unlike others, can without contradiction be lasting yet still historical—as opposed to some less reflective academic views. They either claim, as Hegel and Nietzsche do, that we are at the final point of serious change or have closed the circle, or they examine the very intelligibility of time and identity that makes "contradiction" meaningful.

33. Consider my discussion of reverence in the next chapter. See also Mark Blitz, "Some Notes on Religion and Democratic Liberty," *Krakowskie Studia Miedzynarodowe* 2 (2011): 67–74.

34. Claims that different languages open us to different views of what is are subject to these same problems of showing clearly just what could not have been seen by others, or why what some language makes it difficult to notice and state is not a failing of that language rather than a virtue.

35. For Heidegger generally, consider, among others, Mark Blitz, *Heidegger's "Being and Time" and the Possibility of Political Philosophy*, with a New Afterword (Philadelphia: Paul Dry Books, 2017; orig. Cornell University Press, 1981); Alexander Duff, *Heidegger and Politics* (Cambridge: Cambridge University Press, 2015); Theodore Kisiel, *The Genesis of Heidegger's "Being and Time"* (Berkeley: University of California Press, 1993); Richard Polt, *Heidegger: An Introduction* (Ithaca, NY: Cornell University Press, 1999); and Thomas Sheehan, *Making Sense of Heidegger* (Lanham, MD: Rowman and Littlefield, 2015).

CHAPTER TWO.   The Nature of Freedom and Rights

1. If to be free is to be unburdened, light, not oppressed, not being free means to be closed, pushed, or burdened, or to be buffeted arbitrarily.

2. See Isaiah Berlin, "Two Concepts of Liberty," in *Four Essays on Liberty* (Oxford: Oxford University Press, 1969), 118–72; and Mark Blitz, "An Affirmative Defense of the Liberal Tradition," *Law and Liberty*, February 23, 2015. For various contemporary discussions of freedom, see David Schmidtz and Carmen Pavel, eds., *The Oxford Handbook of Freedom* (New York: Oxford University Press, 2018). See also Jacob Klein, *Lectures and Essays*, ed. Robert B. Williamson and Elliott Zuckerman (Annapolis, MD: St. John's College Press, 1985), ch. 7, "The Problem of Freedom."

3. Consider act I, scene 2, of Shakespeare's *Henry V*.

4. Thinking, as well as acting, usually takes for granted a context of intelligibility that, once exposed, often answers a supposed question, dissolves a supposed paradox, or allows wider and deeper reflection.

5. See Locke, *An Essay Concerning Human Understanding*; and Thomas Jefferson, Declaration of Independence.

6. Consider Hobbes, *Leviathan*; and Alexis de Tocqueville, *Democracy in America*, ed. and trans. Harvey C. Mansfield and Delba Winthrop (Chicago: University of Chicago Press, 2000), vol. 2, pt. 2, chs. 10–16. *Democracy in America* was first published in French, 1835, 1840.

7. Freedom is self-gathering, as "self" is understood in a way of life, for goods in that way of life as connected to the understanding of goodness that allows them to be good, and nonhindrance and self-direction for the particular goods one wishes or chooses. Hindrance is in terms of a direction

or binding direction; the direction or continuity is what is hindered. Both hindrance and direction are first meaningful and stand within the goodness of the goal, the intelligibility of the steps to it that one is taking and is permitted to take, and the way of life overall. Full freedom would thus be full gatheredness and full openness in full meaning (full intelligibility and guidingness), i.e., in the most complete proper movements among the most fully independent and wholly connected parts. And it would be the fullest self-direction and unhinderedness in the fullest concrete activities within this meaning—e.g., the use of our powers of soul and reason to understand the whole of what is. The good use of our powers ultimately strives for an upward perfection and not only an ongoing satisfaction.

8. On emergence, see Sean Carroll, *Something Deeply Hidden* (New York: Dutton, 2019), 234–39.

9. For this discussion, the difference between simple determinism and the unmatched or effectively perfect predictive power of quantum mechanics is not relevant. See Bernhard L. Trout, "Quantum Mechanics and Political Philosophy," in *Mastery of Nature*, ed. Svetozar Y. Minkov and Bernhardt Trout (Philadelphia: University of Pennsylvania Press, 2018), 230.

10. From this point of view, Kant's split between moral freedom and natural causes seems compelling. See, too, Trout's article in Minkov and Trout, *Mastery of Nature*. For this topic, also consider Svetozar Y. Minkov, *Leo Strauss on Science* (Albany: SUNY Press, 2016); and Jerry Weinberger, *Science, Faith, and Politics: Francis Bacon and the Utopian Roots of the Modern Age* (Ithaca, NY: Cornell University Press, 1985).

11. Heidegger, *Zollikon Seminars*, 155.

12. Ibid., 217.

13. Ibid., 186.

14. Ibid., 196.

15. Ibid., 217; my emphasis. I have critically considered other elements of Heidegger's views earlier and will do so also in what follows.

16. If this "bringing out" or revealing is central, in what way can it be guided? We can be guided only if we understand being guided and, thus, only if we understand the human. We are, therefore, ultimately guided by the fullest and most comprehensive bringing out of the human, and other things' powers in relation to this, while also allowing what stands on its own to flourish. We cannot accomplish this with indisputable knowledge or unquestionable consistency. I will address these limits in my final chapter.

17. Consider Paul Ricoeur, *Interpretation Theory: Discourse and the Surplus of Meaning* (Fort Worth: Texas Christian University Press, 1976).

18. In a formal sense this view is common among Plato, Hegel, Heidegger, and Locke. Much of this issue depends on how concrete choices that

seem to limit freedom also expand it—from Hegel's dialectical oppositions to Plato's images to Heidegger's authentic openness to, immersion in, and projection of the horizon of being.

19. See Peter Augustine Lawler, *The Restless Mind* (Lanham, MD: Rowman and Littlefield, 1993).

20. See Aristotle, *Nicomachean Ethics*, trans. Robert Bartlett and Susan Collins (Chicago: University of Chicago Press, 2011).

21. Consider Hobbes's discussion of celerity, steady direction, and other intellectual virtues in chapter 8 of the *Leviathan*; and Wittgenstein's view of understanding as being able to "go on." Ludwig Wittgenstein, *Philosophical Investigations*, trans. G. E. M. Anscombe (London: Blackwell, 1953), sec. 151.

22. Movements are experienced, felt, but also seen because they separate and are separated as well as combining and being combined. Cf. Plato's discussion of pleasure in the *Philebus*. Seth Benardete, trans., *The Tragedy and Comedy of Life: Plato's "Philebus"* (Chicago: University of Chicago Press, 1993).

23. See Plato's *Republic*, *Symposium*, and *Phaedrus*. Plato's *"Symposium,"* trans. Seth Benardete, commentary by Seth Benardete and Allan Bloom (Chicago: University of Chicago Press, 2001); Leo Strauss, *On Plato's "Symposium,"* ed. Seth Benardete (Chicago: University of Chicago Press, 2001); *Plato's "Phaedrus,"* trans. James H. Nichols Jr. (Ithaca, NY: Cornell University Press, 1998); David Levy, *Eros and Socratic Political Philosophy* (New York: Palgrave Macmillan, 2013); and Harvey C. Mansfield, *Manliness* (New Haven, CT: Yale University Press, 2006).

24. What one combines with is an imitation or reflection of an idea, so it is precious, yet one joins with it.

25. What is more complete brings out more powers in fuller combinations.

26. Consider Plato's *Symposium*.

27. Spiritedness sees many ones but not with their own features and tends to force or agglomerate them into One intellectually—modern mathematics and science, for example. Politically, an example is conquest followed by destruction or full assimilation. Or spiritedness sees each as a simple, separate, or recalcitrant one: an enemy or other against whom one must defend oneself if he cannot be conquered; or, intellectually, what appears to be irrational if it cannot be mastered. Spiritedness's problem is one and many. Eros sees wholes, with their own features, but then larger wholes, combinations, the Whole. Or it remains with the exquisite independence of each whole, or parts as whole, each beauty, each wholeness. Its problem is whole and part. Thumos's parts are or tend to be ones, and eros's parts are or tend to be wholes. See Plato's *Republic*.

28. Eros and thumos are also connected to wonder and perplexity. The satisfaction of wonder is to gaze at the complete or what seems complete but then also to join and combine with it, e.g., in understanding, love, or educating personally or politically, and to elevate, perfect, and widen oneself, seeing seeming wholes as imperfect appearances but also still seeing how each is a whole—combinations as wholes, then greater wholes. The satisfaction of perplexity is solving and resolving for oneself, seeing how what is separate or independent can be universalized, dissolving difficulties, conquering, mastering (not gazing), protecting politically and personally (children, one's own). But ultimately it is also seeing how the perplexity's subject still remains independent, how it is a one as well as one of a universal. Because eros, thumos, and the intellect are linked, all are connected to meaning as intelligible and guiding. There is a continuing, if never fully resolved, dialectic of combining and independence.

29. In eros one might not combine because one sees oneself as too pure and exquisite or as too humble and unworthy, that is, as too perfect or imperfect. In excess or licentiousness one sees oneself as too complete—I am only or primarily this characteristic—or as too needy—only one good matters. So one does not see oneself or others properly as wholes and parts of wholes. In thumos one might see oneself as too "proud" (i.e., arrogant) or too fearful to be or allow others to be independent.

30. As I have suggested, other views of goodness are also inherent in this view and we can therefore ultimately compare them.

31. Consider Locke, *Two Treatises of Government*.

32. Consider Hugh Heclo, *On Thinking Institutionally* (Boulder, CO: Paradigm Publishers, 2008).

33. Consider Plato's *Gorgias. Plato's "Gorgias,"* trans. James H. Nichols Jr. (Ithaca, NY: Cornell University Press, 1998); and Blitz, *Conserving Liberty*.

34. Consider for the question of virtue and prudence in a republic various discussions by Publius in *The Federalist Papers*, e.g., Nos. 10, 37, 63, and 70. *The Federalist Papers*, ed. Clinton Rossiter, introd. Charles Kesler (New York: Signet, 2003).

35. See Locke's *Two Treatises*; and Aristotle's discussion of kingship in the *Politics*. Aristotle, *Politics*, trans. Carnes Lord (Chicago: University of Chicago Press, 2013).

36. For a discussion of legitimacy where it means justified rule more broadly, see Clyde H. Ray, *John Marshall's Constitutionalism* (Albany: SUNY Press, 2019), ch. 1.

37. Consider especially the first of Locke's *Two Treatises* and his *Essay Concerning Human Understanding*, bk. IV.

38. The three sections of Hegel's *Philosophy of Right* follow this direction.

39. Mastery shapes, places, and arranges rather than seeks or follows someone else's order or a natural order.

40. The body is an enlivening, a shaping of things that brings out their meaning, a forming by and expression of my powers and properties. It is not as such my identity.

41. The dialectic of the separate "I" and then reaching out, or the immersed "I" and then pulling back or separating, may finally seek to reach the true whole. The movement in thinking's most meaningful separating and combining would most centrally define "I."

42. Seeming, because actual reverent ceremonies have something conventional if not pretentious about them.

43. See my earlier discussion of perplexity and wonder.

44. "And for the support of this Declaration, with firm reliance on the protection of divine Providence, we mutually pledge to each other our Lives, our Fortunes and our sacred Honor." Jefferson, Declaration of Independence.

45. The holy is not identical to what is pious, if by acting piously we mean walking along an orthodox path. This can involve ways of life and "traditions" and not merely gods directly.

46. See Locke's *Second Treatise*, ch. 5; and Hegel's *Philosophy of Right*, pt. 1, sec. 1.

47. Goods are hunted as well as sought.

48. See *The Federalist Papers*, Nos. 25, 49, and 62.

49. I develop these preliminary remarks at greater length below.

CHAPTER THREE.   The Nature of Power and Property

1. Consider Aristotle, *Metaphysics*, trans. Joe Sachs (Santa Fe, NM: Green Lion Press, 1999); Christopher Bruell, *Aristotle as Teacher* (South Bend, IN: St. Augustine's Press, 2014); Martin Heidegger, *Aristotle's Metaphysics 1–3*, trans. Walter Brogan and Peter Warneck (Evanston, IL: Northwestern University Press, 1995), first published in German in 1981 from a lecture course delivered in 1931; Plato, *Sophist*, trans. Seth Benardete (Chicago: University of Chicago Press, 1986); Hobbes, *Leviathan*; Locke, *Essay Concerning Human Understanding*; Nietzsche, *Beyond Good and Evil*; and Martin Heidegger, *Nietzsche* (Pfullingen: Neske, 1961).

2. See my earlier discussion of movement.

3. Consider, e.g., an awesome presence.

4. The power to do x must also mean that x and power first need to come forward in a certain way—for example, in Hobbes, as a means to an end: power as any means that can make something happen or relieve unease indicates that desire, satisfaction, and means must approach us in this general way.

5. See Plato, *Sophist*, 247d-e; Aristotle, *Metaphysics*, bk. 5, ch. 12, bk. 9; Locke, *Essay Concerning Human Understanding*, II, 21; and Hobbes, *Leviathan*, ch. 10.

6. What shapes or forms places in order or sees and brings out an order that is already there. Mere containing (when not a synonym for shaping) does not. Things contained are not formed, or they are broken down and re-formed.

7. Humans have a great range of the powers of other animals, naturally and technologically. We can swim, fly, race, build, growl, tweet, etc. We are the "animal" par excellence. This does not mean, however, that we are animals onto whom reason is stitched as an extra quality. Rather, our distinctive and dominant power forms the rest, as our soul organizes and gives purpose and direction to our body but does not control it completely. Consider for this question the divisions and discussions in Plato's *Statesman*, esp. 261b-266c.

8. See Plato's *Republic* and *Gorgias*; Aristotle's *Politics*, bk. 5, chs. 10 and 11; and Xenophon's *Hiero*. Consider Leo Strauss, *On Tyranny*, ed. Victor Gourevitch and Michael Roth (Chicago: University of Chicago Press, 2013); and Mark Blitz, "Tyranny Ancient and Modern," in *Confronting Tyranny*, ed. Tovio Koivukoski and David Tabachnik (Lanham, MD: Rowman and Littlefield, 2005).

9. So: courage is proper separating or protecting, often through (proper) force.

10. The powerful serve does this to the ball.

11. "Not excessive" can for the moment be great—the overwhelming beauty of powerful music, for example.

12. Examples of this are the misuse of animals and the kind of unlocking of energy from rivers that distorts the landscape.

13. See Plato's *Republic* and *Statesman*, 291a-297e. For discussions of the basis of modern political institutions, see Harvey C. Mansfield, *Statesmanship and Party Government: A Study of Burke and Bolingbroke* (Chicago: University of Chicago Press, 1965); and Harvey C. Mansfield Jr., *Taming the Prince: The Ambivalence of Modern Executive Power* (New York: Free Press, 1989).

14. See Leo Strauss, *What Is Political Philosophy?* (Glencoe, IL: Free Press, 1959); Leo Strauss, *Liberalism, Ancient and Modern* (New York: Basic Books, 1968); and Mark Blitz, "Hegel and Progressivism," *Krakowskie Studia*

Miedzynarodowe 2 (2009): 293–307. "In Machiavelli's teaching we have the first example of a spectacle which has renewed itself in almost every generation since. . . . An amazing contraction of the horizon presents itself as an amazing enlargement of the horizon" (*What Is Political Philosophy?*, 43).

15. Is power as strength always connected to spiritedness? Yes, as concentration and separation and as an incorporating that does not keep parts as parts or make a new whole. In Nietzsche, however, a version of spiritedness also replaces the independent abilities that spiritedness may protect or free.

16. Consider Nietzsche's discussions in *Beyond Good and Evil* and *Twilight of the Idols*, e.g., *Beyond* no. 258 and *Twilight* nos. 37–39. Friedrich Nietzsche, *Twilight of the Idols*, trans. R. J. Hollingwood (Baltimore, MD: Penguin Books, 1968), first published in German in 1889. See also Martin Heidegger, *The History of Being*, trans. William McNeill and Jeffrey Powell (Bloomington: Indiana University Press, 2015), 54–71, 151–67, first published in German in 1998 and written in 1939–40.

17. See Plato's *Republic*, bk. 9; and *Gorgias*. The classical analysis of tyranny in Xenophon, Plato, and Aristotle covers all the major questions of tyranny, as long as one adds the possible use of philosophy for politics, e.g., in Christianity, and Marxist and other ideologies. This question is explored in Xenophon's *Hiero* as well as in the link between the tyrant and the philosopher that Plato considers in the *Republic*.

18. Consider Socrates's discussion with the rhapsode Ion in Plato's *Ion*. Plato, *Ion*, trans. Allan Bloom, in Pangle, *The Roots of Political Philosophy*.

19. Virtue is largely knowledge.

20. See Plato, *Philebus*.

21. See Plato, *Philebus*, as well as Plato's distinction between necessary and unnecessary desires in *Republic*, bk. 8; and Blitz, *Plato's Political Philosophy*. My discussion of pleasure is an example of separating a phenomenon from different regimes in order to compare views of it. Yet my discussion also has in mind specific examples visible more in some regimes than others in order to indicate pleasure's characteristics and the range of goods with which it deals. In this way, a discussion of pleasure (or other phenomena) is reintegrated into an understanding of the various ways of life.

22. Common terms point to common judgment or to commensurability in terms of what is fullest—not a mechanical mathematical measure, however, but rather something akin to what we see in Aristotle's *Ethics* and Plato's *Republic*. It is the measure of and comparison of wholeness, fit, beauty. I will continue the discussion of virtue in later chapters.

23. Consider here the case of Kelo v. City of New London, 545 U.S. 469 (2005). See, in general, Aristotle's *Ethics*, bk. 5.

24. Consider also Plato's *Statesman*, 295c-e.

25. As opposed to our artificial separation of the same power.

26. See also Hegel, *Philosophy of Right*, nos. 41–71; and my earlier discussion of the body

27. Locke, *Second Treatise*, no. 34, in *Two Treatises*.

28. Cf. Heidegger, *Zollikon Seminars*.

29. See Hegel, *Philosophy of Right*, nos. 90–103 (Coercion and Crime).

30. Distinctions sometimes connote excellence, what separates something from others like it: "He is a man of distinction."

CHAPTER FOUR.   The Nature of Virtue

1. For essays that cover much of the material in recent discussions in ethical theory, consider David Copp, ed., *The Oxford Handbook of Ethical Theory* (New York: Oxford University Press, 2005); and Daniel C. Russell, ed., *The Cambridge Companion to Virtue Ethics* (Cambridge: Cambridge University Press, 2013).

2. Consider the discussions of Plato's dialogues in Blitz, *Plato's Political Philosophy*; and Catherine Zuckert, *Plato's Philosophers* (Chicago: University of Chicago Press, 2009). See also the Oxford bibliography of Plato's political thought.

3. I begin with Aristotle, not Plato, because Plato less clearly differentiates virtue in this way. For Aristotle generally, consider, among others, Ronna Burger, *Aristotle's Dialogue with Socrates* (Chicago: University of Chicago Press, 2008); Thomas Pangle, *Aristotle's Teaching in the "Politics"* (Chicago: University of Chicago Press, 2013); and Delba Winthrop, *Aristotle: Democracy and Political Science* (Chicago: University of Chicago Press, 2018).

4. Consider my earlier discussion of power.

5. Consider my earlier discussion of virtue and power.

6. This is why the wish for absolutely obligatory natural laws sacrifices freedom on the altar of tranquillity or certainty.

7. This orients courage to victory. See Plato's *Laches*.

8. Consider my first chapter.

9. Both tolerance and, especially, piety have within them, ready to be brought to the surface in discussion, the question of what holiness and piety truly are.

10. Decline in the importance of the liberal virtues goes hand in hand with the changing understanding within liberal democratic "culture" of the meaning of freedom and of liberal democracy itself. For further discussion of the liberal virtues, see Mark Blitz, *Duty Bound: Responsibility and American Public Life* (Lanham, MD: Rowman and Littlefield, 2005).

11. Consider my recent discussion of justice and property.

12. Goods are necessary only in order to be just.

13. See the discussion of the *Philebus* in Blitz, *Plato's Political Philosophy*.

14. This becomes evident in Kant's and, especially, Hegel's political writings. See Immanuel Kant, *Groundwork of the Metaphysics of Morals* and *Toward Perpetual Peace*, in *Critique of Practical Reason and Other Writings*, ed. Mary J. Gregor (Cambridge: Cambridge University Press, 1996); and Hegel, *Philosophy of Right*. For Kant generally, consider, among others, Paul Guyer, ed., *The Oxford Companion to Kant* (Cambridge: Cambridge University Press, 1992); Heidegger, *Being and Time*; Martin Heidegger, *Phenomenological Interpretation of Kant's "Critique of Pure Reason,"* trans. Parvis Emad and Kenneth Maly (Bloomington: Indiana University Press, 1997), a lecture course delivered in 1927–28 and first published in German in 1977; Susan Meld Shell, *Kant and the Limits of Autonomy* (Cambridge, MA: Harvard University Press), 2009; and Richard L. Velkley, *Freedom and the End of Reason* (Chicago: University of Chicago Press), 1989.

15. For further development of these questions, see Mark Blitz, "Basic Issues in Kant's Moral and Political Thought," *Political Science Reviewer* 30 (2001): 103–19.

16. Consider the development of the state, the so-called *Rechtsstaat*, in Germany in the nineteenth century. See Judith Shklar, *Legalism* (Cambridge, MA: Harvard University Press, 1986).

17. And this openness points ultimately to philosophy and the philosophical life, as I suggested earlier.

18. See Plato's several considerations of the virtues in the *Laches, Charmides, Theages, Republic, Statesman, Gorgias, Meno, Protagoras, Lysis,* and *Euthydemus*. Plato, *"Protagoras" and "Meno,"* trans. Robert C. Bartlett (Ithaca, NY: Cornell University Press, 2004); David Bolotin, *Plato's Dialogue on Friendship: An Interpretation of the "Lysis," with a New Translation* (Ithaca, NY: Cornell University Press, 1979); Plato, *Euthydemus*, trans. Gregory A. McBrayer and Mary Nichols (Newburyport, MA: Focus Publishing, 2011).

19. To be attractive or pleasant, fitting, and strikingly independent are the central characteristics of what is beautiful.

20. Where proper human action is our righteous way, the problems or phenomena that open to the general, and which ultimately can be seen to reflect it, are largely or almost fully hidden, and our way in relation to a fuller way is obscured.

21. This natural generality also limits the power of any authoritative particular "gods."

22. Identity also involves differentiating myself from others: this belongs primarily to my spiritedness—my recognized feeling of spirited movement—

and my erotic reaching out. This differentiating further belongs in practice to my and others seeing my bodily separateness, movement, and possessions, although it is the soul, not the body as such, that is the heart of identity. Identity also involves continuity. Such continuity belongs to my projection—my movement and understanding—outward and what I carry along with me as the base I protect from which I project. A shrinking base and projection is why I may shrink, as it were, as memory and aspiration fade, although "I" am still "I," and this shrinking is a chief reason that others can say that someone is no longer himself even after he can no longer see this himself. (Being no longer oneself is one way one is not oneself. The other is to depart from one's usual characteristics.) Memory is significant as a mechanism of identity, but it is what is remembered and can be recalled that is its heart. Heidegger's notions of thrownness, projection, and immersion are useful for understanding identity and involve one's thrown beginning, the projection of one's own dying—the possible impossibility of all one's possibilities—and one's free authentic resolve. But one must also consider that one's aspiration also orients oneself above oneself.

23. The erotic out to (or "transcending") of one's soul is toward what beckons as good or beautiful. The new whole to which I then belong may lead to an expanded "one," which is the spirited experience of the new whole, now as ours or mine, as one. The back to (or "returning") is to oneself as enclosed or newly enclosed. This "one" can then (seek to) belong to a more complete whole as the (more) beautiful (continues to) beckon, and on and on, given that I am always eros, spiritedness, and reason (speech) together.

CHAPTER FIVE.   The Nature of What Is Common

1. I have emphasized differences, but there are also broadly general practices, similarities as well as differences, in how we see and then deal with, say, infants, young children, and basic necessities in various ways of life. I have mentioned this earlier and will discuss this more fully later in this chapter.

2. In a chain, each link can (usually) be anywhere.

3. Unlike shadows and model airplanes, or Plato's ideas, family resemblances do not suggest the true or perfect instance, with the imitations common to it being inferiors. At most one might be able to discover the first member, although one would need to look at later ones to see which of their features turn out to belong to the family.

4. This statement does not address how a given model organizes, unifies, or links its images.

5. For the question of what is whole or common, consider Plato's *Parmenides*; and Leo Strauss's discussion of homogeneity and heterogeneity in the title essay of *What Is Political Philosophy?* (38–40). *Plato's "Parmenides,"* trans. Albert Keith Whitaker (Newburyport, MA: Focus Publishing, 1996.)

6. This likeness may mean that they are images, copies, bear family resemblances, or are identical members of a universal.

7. More important parts may receive more—more wealth, honor, rule, or "worship." But they may also receive only equal honor and rule, for example, when they are voters or jurors in a democracy, have equal expectations and trust, receive equal treatment under law, and are equally devoted to and protective of this one, this community.

8. Consider Plato's *eide* here.

9. Most superior trios and quartets are not composed of the most outstanding soloists, but such soloists do sometimes come together with excellent results.

10. "Leaders"—coaches and conductors—need to bring things together, which is why the outcome—the victory or successful performance—is theirs a bit more than the participants'.

11. The character that defines this purpose, in turn, is employed in the practice of governing.

12. Consider the discussion in Hegel's *Philosophy of Right*.

13. They are also subtle because each part also participates in its function taken separately (as violinists may play successfully outside this orchestra or any orchestra), and each whole participates in the others (as orchestras are like other orchestras, who may be their competitors).

14. Consider Hobbes's and Locke's discussion of the state of nature.

15. For Machiavelli's thought, consider, among others, Harvey Mansfield Jr., *Machiavelli's New Modes and Orders* (Ithaca, NY: Cornell University Press, 1979); Harvey C. Mansfield, *Machiavelli's Virtue* (Chicago: University of Chicago Press, 1996); Leo Strauss, *Thoughts on Machiavelli* (Glencoe, IL: Free Press, 1958); Catherine H. Zuckert, *Machiavelli's Politics* (Chicago: University of Chicago Press, 2017); and the commentary by Christopher Lynch to his translation of Machiavelli's *Art of War: Niccolò Machiavelli, Art of War*, trans. and ed. and with commentary by Christopher Lynch (Chicago: University of Chicago Press, 2003).

16. They also differ from the whole and good simply that are objects of Platonic inquiry.

17. Consider Rousseau's *The Social Contract, Government of Poland*, and the *Constitutional Project for Corsica*, all in Jean-Jacques Rousseau, *Political Writings*, ed. and trans. Frederick Watkins (Edinburgh: Thomas Nelson and Sons, 1953); G. W. F. Hegel, *Lectures on the Philosophy of World*

History, trans. H. W. Nisbet (Cambridge: Cambridge University Press, 1975); Nietzsche, *Beyond Good and Evil*; and Woodrow Wilson's Fourteen Points (see, e.g., www.u-s-history.com). See also, for several of the issues discussed in this and the following sections, Michael Walzer, *Thick and Thin* (Notre Dame, IN: University of Notre Dame Press, 2019); and the discussion and references in Ray, *John Marshall's Constitutionalism*, ch. 4.

18. Historically variable dominant drives are what Nietzsche has in mind with different races. See *Beyond Good and Evil*, pref. and pt. 8, "Peoples and Fatherlands"; and *Twilight of the Idols*.

19. See Blitz, *Heidegger's "Being and Time" and the Possibility of Political Philosophy*.

20. This view is an element of Heidegger's association with the Nazis and their attempted "coordination" of all professions and activities.

21. See the beginning of Plato's *Greater Hippias*. Plato, *Greater Hippias*, trans. David R. Sweet, in Pangle, *The Roots of Political Philosophy*.

22. Consider several of Plato's dialogues, e.g., the beginning of the *Laws* and *Greater Hippias*.

23. This variety is naturally explicable, as I am describing it here and have discussed it previously.

24. To be liberated from unreasonable claims of revelation, and remain free from unreasonable epistemological tangles, it is useful to clarify the everyday differences between the dream world and the real or waking world, with which the dream world is contrasted commonsensically. To discuss these differences comprehensively would take us too far afield, but I can indicate the major elements that mark their difference: lack of continuity between what occurs in a dream and effects in the waking world; inability to continue to master skills or enjoy goods one believes one has mastered or accumulated in dreams; dreams' lack of sustained progressive interrelations with each other; the inability to reproduce or demonstrate much of dreams' content and experiences for others; and the partialness of the sensory and other qualities we experience in dreams. Dreams may share meaning with the waking world, but they lack the full powers connected to that meaning.

25. Consider Plato's *Laws* and *Republic*; Aristotle's *Politics*, bks. 7 and 8; and Machiavelli's *Prince* and *Discourses*. Niccolò Machiavelli, *The Prince*, trans. Harvey C. Mansfield Jr. (Chicago: University of Chicago Press, 1998); Niccolò Machiavelli, *Discourses on Livy*, trans. Harvey Mansfield Jr. and Nathan Tarcov (Chicago: University of Chicago Press, 1996).

26. Consider also Plato's *Statesman*.

27. See Blitz, *Conserving Liberty*.

28. The events of birth, marriage, and death are central to our grasp of what is inviolable in human beings, and to our recognizing our ability to

make the best of ourselves. Religious ritual may consecrate these events and harness their emotional power and seriousness. It may also offer consolation that implicitly recognizes the limits that belong to what is choiceworthy.

29. Consider also my earlier discussion of property and the body.

CHAPTER SIX.   The Nature of Goods

1. Substantively, the guidance and sufficiency that characterize what is good for human beings take their direction from satisfaction in the fullest case, the philosophical case. The fullest use of the intellect is oriented to and involves pleasure, completeness, and purity. What is fulfilling or satisfying here and now, in this activity and community, reflects the fullest, more purely intellectual case. As Socrates suggests in the *Republic*, we each seek what is good but cannot grasp it sufficiently (505d-e). My argument is that theory (philosophy) and the highest practice (statesmanship) show an excellence that is reasonably clear. The other activities are declensions from virtue, justice, and the noble as they exist more completely.

2. Freedom from religion, indeed, is often allied with an upsurge in attraction to pleasure. See Leo Strauss, *Spinoza's Critique of Religion* (New York: Schocken Books, 1965) and *Philosophy and Law*, trans. Eve Adler (Albany: SUNY Press, 1995), and the chapter "Notes on Lucretius" in Strauss's *Liberalism, Ancient and Modern*.

3. One might consider intellectual pleasure in these terms, where wonder (as admiring) is a burgeoning that may then issue in completeness or sufficiency and in precise knowledge as exquisite or refined, and perplexity is a need but not an emptiness. Rather, it is "need" (spur, drive, incentive) as seeking to master (as one masters or cuts through a problem) or possess, an occasion to test competence and to experience pleasure as momentum, intensity, unification, and expansion, which also issues in a form of satisfaction and precision.

4. Even the virtue of moderation is complex in this way because it both enjoys sensual pleasure and, as a virtue, experiences the different, nonsensual, pleasure of virtuous action itself.

5. See Kant's *Groundwork of the Metaphysics of Morals*, sec. II.

6. See Plato's *Gorgias*. Attempts to ignore what we are and become shells of ourselves, in fact show what we are.

7. See Aristotle's discussion in the *Politics* of the relation between the rule of the best laws and the best man.

8. This view might become explicit in certain circumstances—choosing laws or constitution making, as I discussed these earlier.

9. Consider in this regard my earlier discussion of history. One may argue that religious ways do not as such permit the freedom to seek relentlessly, or grasp conceptually, the full meaning and excellence of the virtues, goods, and pleasures they control. In such ways, my own, our own, and what is good are tied together too strictly for complete conceptualization; they do not within themselves allow the distance that questions their way. Still, the basis and the possibility for questioning must and does exist in these ways, as I indicated in discussions of individual pleasure, dreams, and other matters. Also consider here Benjamin I. Schwartz, *The World of Thought in Ancient China* (Cambridge, MA: Harvard University Press, 1985), 78–79, and the chapter on Confucius generally.

10. See Plato, *Philebus* 64d-66d and *Statesman* 283c-285c.

11. Consider my earlier brief discussions of war and victory.

12. Consider Winston Churchill's interest in technology throughout his career, and the place of technology in war generally and in the Second World War in particular.

13. Unless a defense of equal freedom for rational beings is incorrect either in terms of equal rights or Kant's universalism, moreover, justice would demand a kind of equal treatment for rational beings—us as well as our possible rational superiors, whatever the differences in power.

14. For several of these issues, see Yuval Noah Harari, *Homo Deus* (New York: HarperCollins, 2017).

15. See Plato's discussion in bk. 6 of the *Republic* of the divided line.

16. Consider the relation between John Locke and the founding of the United States.

17. Consider Nietzsche's claim in *Beyond Good and Evil* that Christianity is Platonism for the people; and Plato's dialogue, the *Euthyphro*.

18. The artist was earlier an important but not exemplary figure. Consider Plato's *Republic* and *Symposium*, for example.

19. Consider Leo Strauss's *On Tyranny* and his discussion there with Alexandre Kojève.

MARK BLITZ is the Fletcher Jones Professor of Political Philosophy at Claremont McKenna College. He is the author of numerous books, including *Conserving Liberty, Plato's Political Philosophy,* and *Duty Bound: Responsibility and American Public Life.*

CPSIA information can be obtained
at www.ICGtesting.com
Printed in the USA
LVHW080050250221
679848LV00006B/74